furniture
RESTORATION

A professional at work

furniture RESTORATION

A professional at work

John Lloyd

GUILD OF MASTER CRAFTSMAN PUBLICATIONS

First published 2001 by
Guild of Master Craftsman Publications Ltd
Castle Place, 166 High Street,
Lewes, East Sussex BN7 1XU

Text © John Lloyd 2001
© in the work GMC Publications 2001
Photographs by Chris Skarbon (frontispiece, pp vi, 24,37,65,94,103)
and by the author

ISBN 1 86108 220 7

A catalogue record for this book is available from the British Library.

Cover designed by Ian Smith

Set in Garamond and Franklin Gothic

Printed and bound by Kyodo Printing (Singapore) under the supervision of
MRM Graphics, Winslow, Buckinghamshire, UK

SAFETY

Furniture restoration should not be a dangerous activity, provided that sensible precautions are taken to avoid unnecessary risk.

Always ensure that work is securely held in a suitable clamp or other device, and that the workplace lighting is adequate.

Keep tools sharp; blunt tools are dangerous because they require more pressure and may behave unpredictably. Store them so that you, and others, cannot touch their cutting edges accidentally.

Be particular about disposing of shavings, finishing materials, oily rags, etc., which may be a fire hazard.

Do not work when your concentration is impaired by drugs, alcohol or fatigue.

Do not remove safety guards from power tools; pay attention to electrical safety.

The safety advice in this book is intended for your guidance, but cannot cover every eventuality: the safe use of hand and power tools is the responsibility of the user. If you are unhappy with a particular technique or procedure, do not use it – there is always another way.

CONTENTS

INTRODUCTION 1

1 A RESTORER'S TALE *rescuing a badly repaired tea-table* 3

2 WORKING THE MAGIC *tambours and cylinders* 7

3 WRITING WRONGS *restoring a rosewood writing table* 11

4 USE AND ABUSE *a George III chest of drawers* 15

5 ON THE EDGE *cockbeading on drawer fronts* 18

6 FORTIFICATION OF A PIANOFORTE *restoring a square piano* 20

7 SOFA, SO GOOD *a mahogany sofa table* 25

8 ALMOST A COPY *copying period chairs* 29

9 COPIES COMPLETE *finishing the duplicated chairs* 32

10 TEA-TABLE TROUBLES BREWING *an 18th century tripod table* 38

11 RESTORING A LUNCHTIME DRAMA *a mahogany Chippendale-style carver* 42

12 WHEN CABINETS TOOK SILK *a spectacular Regency chiffonier* 45

13 FLY LEG IN WIND *putting a leg to rights* 49

14 GRINS AND GRIMACES *taking the kinks out of a card table* 53

15 A STITCH IN TIME *a 17th century oak food hutch* 57

16 UNDER THE WEATHER *a 'dial' or 'banjo' barometer* 61

17 ACCORDING TO THE RULE *a Pembroke table with rule joint* 66

18 A PARTRIDGE IN A PIER TABLE *a rosewood console table* 70

19 A CENTURY SINCE *Victorian furniture* 74

20 ALL THE CARDS ON THE TABLE *a rosewood and coromandel card table* 78

21 AFTER THE BODGERS *saving a chair from an uncertain future* 82

22 INGENIOUS CABINET MAKER *a salute to Gillows craftsmanship* 86

23 CLEVER CURES *an 18th century chest on chest* 90

24 CRAMPING YOUR STYLE *getting to grips with glueing* 95

25 RESTORER WITH CRAMP *making your own ingenious devices* 99

26 FROM BUNS TO CABRIOLES *restoring a chest on stand* 104

27 CAT SCRATCH FEVER *a Pembroke table damaged by claws* 108

28 WHEN GRANDFATHER IS NOT A GRANDFATHER *repairing a longcase clock* 112

29 OUT OF JOINT *saying no to biscuits* 116

INDEX 120

METRIC CONVERSION TABLE 121

INTRODUCTION

My first formal foray into the world of woodwork was at school, at the hands of a teacher who had obviously been given rather poor advice by his careers master. His teaching skills were minimal, and a career in the East German Secret Police was obviously a missed opportunity.

My school woodworking classroom was an environment in which sharp tools were considered to be unsuitable things to put in the unskilled hands of 11 year old boys. Trying to change the shape of bits of wood, albeit softwood, with blunt tools was so frustrating that, when given the option, I chose the potentially less mentally damaging and possibly more creatively fulfilling option of metalwork. And there my rather unimpressive career as a wood craftsman ended, to be revived only after many years, out of necessity, because I needed somewhere to hang my clothes. But the gentle art of screwing together lumps of MDF and softwood, which could hardly be described as cabinet making, had a rather strange effect on me. I was enjoying myself enormously, and I found that I was developing a rather bizarre desire to learn the skills of a Georgian cabinetmaker.

In the meantime I had been following a rather haphazard 'career path', with occasional forays into sailing and skiing, and the whole experience, if enjoyable at times, was largely unfulfilling. It wasn't until I had settled down to a proper job complete with company car, mortgage, wife and baby that I decided it was time for my final career move into the world of woodwork. Surprisingly my wife Sara Jane not only agreed to this, but actively encouraged me – unlike many others of my friends and family who probably thought I was a selfish lunatic. Perhaps she was

just sick of seeing that miserable 'desk-bound' look on my face, although little was she to know that this look was soon to be replaced by one of terror as I realised the enormity of what I was taking on.

In an attempt to prove that I was not completely mad, I decided to check my aptitude for my newly chosen career by enrolling on a short cabinet making course at West Dean College in West Sussex, where I was taught by one Bruce Luckhurst. A whole weekend spent sharpening bits of steel to a degree of sharpness I had previously thought was only possible with something with Wilkinson Sword printed on it, was followed by a week of discovering the pure joy of transforming the shape of bits of hardwood with razor sharp tools. I ended the week the proud possessor of a completely useless dovetailed, veneered, crossbanded and inlayed drawer, and an odd collection of extremely sharp second hand tools – and I was completely hooked.

Having discovered Mr Luckhurst's depth of knowledge and remarkable teaching skills, I decided to entrust my future to his hands and enrolled on his furniture restoration course. This involved a year of developing hand skills and cramming information into a brain that thought its days of formal education were long over – twelve hour days in the workshop followed by bookwork in what was left of the day and weekends at home with my family. Having finished the course, and ready to earn the fortune that I had been promising my family, I found myself a bench to rent with an inspiring view of the Bow Flyover, and very soon realised that my training had only just begun.

To my eternal gratitude, Sara Jane continued to support me, and I found people who were willing to entrust their treasured antiques into my not very experienced hands. Now, some years later, the view from my bench has changed from traffic battling its way into the city to sheep grazing in a field, but I still work for some of those original clients, and I'm still continuing the never-ending learning process.

Writing for *Furniture and Cabinetmaking* magazine has become part of the learning process for me. It makes me sit down and consider what I'm doing in the workshop in a way that I would not otherwise do.

Perhaps my ramblings will inspire readers of this book to get some training and eventually become involved in the wonderfully fulfilling process of restoring furniture.

John Lloyd, March, 2001

A restorer's tale

FURNITURE RESTORERS are a dedicated breed – when not actually restoring something they will often be found researching the subject. There is a chap in my workshop who doesn't seem able to eat his sandwiches without a furniture-related book in his hand – this could be aimed at impressing visitors or may be just an aid to digestion.

This kind of behaviour could be mistaken for anorak-like tendencies, although I like to think it shows an insatiable thirst for knowledge. In my own personal quest for cerebral development, I was flicking through *The Shorter Dictionary of English Furniture*, a tome that can be used for enhancing upper-arm muscles as well as developing the mind, when I came across these descriptions under the heading 'Cabinetmakers' – the eminent Thomas Sheraton Esq. observed that the trade was considered 'one of the leading mechanical professions in every polite nation in Europe', which sounds good even if it isn't still the case. Evelyn, in 1664, referred to the development of English cabinetmakers as being 'from very vulgar and pitiful artists, come to produce works as curious for their fitting and admirable for their dexterity in contriving as any we meet with from abroad' – which is probably a compliment.

"Without the vital ingredients of training and an appreciation of the remarkable adhesive properties of animal glue, the only option was more screws from the front!"

LEFT: A table that has had some 'repairs' of a dubious nature

ABOVE: Screw heads do not enhance this piece!

ABOVE RIGHT: Unusual construction of the frieze, coopered with loose tongues and a signature!

Pitiful artist

Sadly, the person who had at some stage repaired a tea-table that we have in the workshop at the moment, had not reached the status of cabinet-maker, or restorer, and was still at the 'very vulgar and pitiful artist' stage of his, or her, development!

Evidence of this is shown by the rather obvious addition of some screws in the front face of the front legs – but to be fair, it looks like they had screwed into the back face of the legs first. This had presumably not had the desired effect, and without the vital ingredients of training and an appreciation of the remarkable adhesive properties of animal glue, the only option was more screws from the front!

Dismantling

Despite all this metalwork, the front legs had, as usual, come loose again and the table's owner was of the opinion that the inlay at the top of the leg would look better without the extra embellishment of random screw heads!

Having removed all the screws, the legs, not surprisingly, fell off. Part of the reason for metal-work in the first place was that the legs had developed splits running vertically down from the bridle joints – and to add to the problem, the construction of the frieze was coming apart in the area of the leg joints.

Looking from the underside of the table it can be seen that the frieze has been constructed using a coopering technique with loose

RIGHT: Leg splits cramped-up and plugs fitted

tongues at each joint, which is a method I have not come across before on this sort of table. It is more usual to find the curved frieze of a demi-lune table such as this one, being built up in brick formation, although I did find an example in 'the tome' of a semi-circular table in oak which was described as the precursor to the fold-over card tea-table. This table has a hinged top and a gated leg to form a circular table when open, and has a carved oak facing only ⅜in thick bent to curve, and nailed in position to form the frieze. Today, you would probably whip out your vacuum bag and laminate it!

Signature

Whilst on the subject of the underside of the table, you can see that some period graffiti has been added – it is of course impossible to say when it was done and the signature certainly isn't that of Mr Chippendale – but this is the sort of thing that people love to see hiding somewhere on a piece of furniture. Even if the writing is illegible and it is unclear when it was done, if it is in a fine flowing copperplate hand it should not be disturbed as it seems to make a piece more desirable and pre-sumably, from a dealer's point of view, more saleable!

The only way to cramp something like this is with a band cramp

Repair

To repair the split in the leg was in fact straightforward – the mating surfaces were remarkably undamaged and little pressure was required to close the joint. It was therefore just a case of introducing some glue into the joint and cramping from both directions to keep the surfaces in register. To repair the screw holes in the front face, I decided to use a combination of cross grain plugs and patches. The plug cutters I use produce a tapered plug and the matching drills are precision point TCT lip and spur bits which came in a set of four sizes. These give a precise fit with no visible glue line.

The drill bits do, however, need something for the central point to stick into to stop them wandering, and the holes therefore must be plugged before they are plugged! To make this exercise a success, an important element, as is true with all patching, is to match the grain of the original surface with that of the plug. This involves rummaging around in all those boxes of offcuts — of which there are many when you are a restorer because you find it impossible to throw anything away!

Having found a suitable piece of wood and cut a perfect plug, the next thing that will make this exercise either a success or a failure is the orientation of the grain. The thing to remember here is that if there is a large amount of plug protruding from the surface you are repairing – the grain which was perfectly aligned when the plug was fitted, will rather annoyingly change direction as you trim the plug flush – so trim plugs to have only a slight protrusion before fitting.

Patches

The next part of this repair is to patch over the relevant parts of the plugs

with some mahogany. Patches should never be fitted with a joint going straight across the grain because it makes it difficult to make them disappear, so in this case the vertical joints which are running with the grain are straight, with the other joints being cut at an angle. The resulting shape is a sort of flat-topped equilateral triangle.

Loose joints

To repair the loose joints in the groundwork of the frieze was just a case of working animal glue into them and cramping them together – but cramping a semi-circle is not easy unless you have a band cramp in your arsenal. The one I used on this occasion is nice and wide and was designed for holding down heavy loads on lorries. It is fitted with a powerful

ratchet mechanism which could easily cause the frieze to implode, so it needed to be handled with care, protecting the surface in contact with the ratchet mechanism, and fitting something around the corners, both to protect them and allow the strap to slide easily around them.

ABOVE: Completed patches to screw-hole repairs

BELOW: Ground-work has had to be repaired for the hinges to be re-mounted

"The secret weapon in this case is a cranked or dog-leg chisel which allows you to trim the patch with a good degree of control, and means that the original surfaces can remain intact"

ABOVE: A cranked chisel is the only way to get to the centre of the table for this cross-banding repair

ABOVE RIGHT: Cutting the stringing using a guillotine action

Hinges

Another part of a fold-over table that invariably requires attention is the area around the hinges. There will often be veneer damage caused by slight, or not so slight, movement in the hinge. Re-securing the hinges will possibly require the screw holes being plugged and the screws being re-fitted, and in some cases, for a bit more of a challenge, the ground work will have to be stabilised — but veneer patches in this area will be rather pointless if the hinge is still flapping about.

On the positive side, the veneer is usually in the form of a cross banding — which means that the repairs are simple because the joins can follow the grain.

Part of the cross-banding in the opened top of this table also required a patch. The patch itself is, once again, not too much of a challenge — but trimming the patch can be a problem because it is in the middle of a large surface which is not terribly accessible with a standard chisel because the handle gets in the way. The secret

RIGHT: Stringing is glued back in place with Scotch glue

weapon in this case is a cranked or dog-leg chisel which allows you to trim the patch with a good degree of control and means that the original surfaces can remain intact.

Stringing

The stringing around the edge of the table needed several repairs but straight joints across the grain will, as usual, result in your being struck by a thunderbolt or a plague of locusts descending upon your workshop – the only way to avoid this is to use nice long scarfe joints.

To cut the scarfe on the stringing requires a big chisel, or failing that, a big plane blade. The cut is made using a sort of guillotine action – put one tip of the blade on the cutting block, hold it vertical, and with one firm

movement slice down through the stringing. Keeping fingertips out of the way is important as red stringing is rarely appropriate!

The line is glued with the hot sticky stuff – the easiest way to hold it in place while the glue sets is with masking tape. It is important to check whether the tape is going to remove any of the original surface around the repair when it is removed — a little test on an inconspicuous spot is a good plan and, in any case, the tape should not be left on for too long.

Finishing

The final challenge, as is always the way, is to colour and polish all the repairs to make them look a little more at home – and this table also needed a light clean and a wax. ∎

"Straight joints across the grain will, as usual, result in your being struck by a thunderbolt or a plague of locusts descending upon your workshop"

"On the positive side, the veneer is usually in the form of a cross banding — which means that the repairs are simple because the joins can follow the grain"

Working the magic

A cabinet, whether it be in the form of a bookcase, a bureau, or just a cupboard of some sort will, by definition, have a big hole or a series of big holes in the front to enable access to its interior. Having created the interior and the big hole, it is often thought to be a good idea to have a system to cover the big hole up – this may be to keep small, or indeed big, fingers out, and if the cover is not see-through it will hide the unholy mess that may be inside, and will give the opportunity for decorative enhancement to the external face.

Covers

There are, of course, several types of cover available to the cabinetmaker – if your life is already full of challenges and you don't need any more, then a straightforward door may be the answer, and if you really don't like surprises and are of the opinion that the hole you have created is not going to change shape or size, the door can be of frame and panel construction as this won't change either.

If, however, you have a dull life and need something that will stretch you a little, or perhaps a lot, you could make a sliding cover made up of a multitude of strips of wood stuck to a piece of fabric, or you could make it cylindrical and devise a way of making it revolve to cover or uncover the interior. ➤

The cabinetmaker who crafted this piece made life hard for himself by including a cylinder, tambour and marquetry!

"If, however, you have a dull life and need something that will stretch you a little, or perhaps a lot, you could make a sliding cover made up of a multitude of strips of wood stuck to a piece of fabric"

ABOVE **A router is used with a simple fence to cut a groove for a splice in the cylinder**

BELOW **A special jig was used to re-glue the fabric to the back of the tambour**

Whole caboodle

➤ The cabinetmaker who created the piece of furniture that I have in the workshop at the moment must have been feeling very unfulfilled, or perhaps had masochistic tendencies – or maybe he was doing it for a dare, because he has incorporated both tambours and a cylinder in one piece of furniture. Tambours and cylinders can be a pointer to quality in a piece of furniture as they both require a higher degree of craftsmanship and would obviously take longer to create than a few doors or a simple fall. There is a chance though, that if you make something of a complex form it may go wrong, and this is very much the case with both of these.

Historical view

Both the tambour and the cylinder were very popular towards the end of the 18th century and were utilised by the likes of Hepplewhite and Sheraton. Hepplewhite, in his guide of 1788, describes desks fitted with tambours as 'very convenient pieces of furniture' but

they seem to have lost favour with the designers fairly quickly, as in Sheraton's Cabinet Dictionary of 1803 they are described as 'almost out of use being both insecure and liable to injury' – he does concede though, that they are appropriate in small pieces that require little strength or security.

Grey hairs

From a furniture restorer's point of view, if a piece of furniture comes into the workshop and it is fitted with tambours or cylinders, there is a very high probability that they will need at least some attention, and there is a high probability that the attention required will be of some great magnitude, and that you will be in possession of a few

more grey hairs at the end of the experience.

Tambour construction

Tambours may be 'vertical' in that they lift upwards, or 'horizontal' where they slide sideways, but both have the same construction, the only difference being in the direction in which they disappear.

Construction is simple – lots of strips of wood are glued next to each other on a piece of fabric with the ends running in grooves or tracks. The grooves may be straight or curved or often a combination of the two – but the curve can only go in one direction and, if the curve is required to be tight, the wooden strips are required to be thin! On the

RIGHT **The tambour required some extra clamping**

BELOW **Interior of the re-furbished tambour, coloured to match**

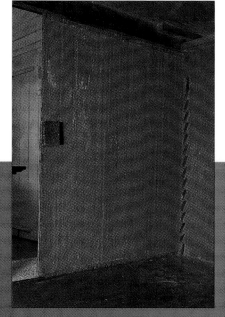

"The construction of a cylinder top relies on coopering technology and problems arise because the cylinder can change shape in that rather annoying way that wood has"

piece I have been working on, the tambours were of the horizontal persuasion and were made up of two separate pieces that met in the middle. Only one required attention and this was because the fabric was torn in several places and some of the wooden strips were trying to get away.

Sick tambour

Dismantling was the first requirement – this meant removing the back boards, and then the invalid was carefully persuaded around the various bends of the track that convey it to the back, the stop was removed, and out it came. A great deal of care was required at this

point as a sick tambour is a rather fragile item! It is a good idea to keep the many strips in order and in any case a jig is required to hold the strips if a new piece of backing fabric is to be fitted. So, before removing the tambour I made up the jig, which consisted of a piece of MDF of a larger dimension than the tambour, and two rebated pieces of wood which fit over the ends of the slats to both hold them down and keep them in line. To keep all the slats fitting snugly against each other I fitted a stop to the base board at one end, and another stop at the other end, with a pair of folding wedges to apply some pressure.

Repair

Having successfully negotiated the patient into the jig, polished side down, I applied some damp kitchen towel to the backing fabric and, having left it to soak, removed the fabric and cleaned off all the old glue. The new piece of fabric was glued on with hide glue, mainly because that is what would have been used, but PVA could be used equally successfully.

It is often the case that the slats are a little less than flat which will mean that the gluing is likely to be unsatisfactory. To counteract this, I made up a piece of MDF of an appropriate size and, having put a piece of silicone baking paper between it and the sticky bit, I pressed the fabric onto the slats. For a successful end result, the glue was not put on too thickly and, when set, I rolled and unrolled it a couple of times to make it flexible and to check that none of the slats had stuck to each other. This done, I added a generous amount of candle wax to the ends of the slats and the running surfaces of the grooves and put it back in its housing to check for its smooth running. If the slat ends or grooves are badly worn, more surgery will be required, but in this case it worked well.

Cylinder construction

The construction of a cylinder top relies on coopering technology and problems arise because the cylinder ➤

LEFT **The polished and re-fitted tambour back in place**

BELOW **Side view showing some magnificent marquetry**

"By pulling out the sliding writing surface the cylinder rotates vertically into the body of the desk as if by magic"

➤ can change shape in that rather annoying way that wood has – and the running groove in the carcass will invariably change its profile due to shrinkage of the carcass sides. This often results in the front edge of the housing breaking out, although in this particular specimen it was not the problem, but there were splits developing along the glue joints of the coopered pieces. Some of these I was able to just clean up and glue together again with the help of a band cramp or two – others could not be coaxed back together and to stabilise these I routed along the line of the joint with the aid of a simple fence, and inserted fillets.

A previous repairer had inserted a butterfly which had, surprise, surprise, failed! The running groove required a little attention to make it the same shape as the cylinder when re-glued, but apart from that it worked quite smoothly.

Magic working

These cylinder tops usually have quite complex linkages that join them to the writing surface of the desk – by pulling out the sliding writing surface the cylinder rotates vertically into the body of the desk as if by magic. Unfortunately the magic wasn't working when the desk arrived at the workshop and judging by the number of screw holes in the fixing area of the mechanism's pivot point, someone had been floundering around trying to find the right spell. This point is quite critical because it is important that when the slide is fully out, the cylinder is right inside the carcass to allow access to the internal drawers. Conversely, it is also a nice touch if the cylinder is completely closed when the slide is right in. To achieve this happy situation requires a cunning plan, a pencil, some paper and some masking tape. I first filled all the existing screw holes and then taped a piece of white paper to cover the likely fixing area, I then fitted the linkages to the slide and the cylinder which were positioned in their respective fully open positions. I covered the back of the pivot pin with pencil and, pushing it against the paper,

marked the arc which the linkage allowed for this position, I then positioned the slide and cylinder in their fully closed positions and again marked the arc of possible positions using the back of the pivot pin. Where the two arcs cross is the point to secure the pivot pin! I suppose it's very obvious really but it had me worried for a minute or two, and I'm sure that as a result my grey hair count has gone up again! ■

Writing wrongs

ABOVE: Regency-style writing table brings elegance to the task

I T WOULD SEEM that we in England were often the last to cotton on to new ideas or designs in furniture. Pieces designed specifically for writing on were in use in Italy and France in the 16th century, but it wasn't until the end of the 17th century, after the Restoration, that writing tables or desks were made in England – it wasn't that we didn't write, we just didn't feel it necessary to write in style! And just to rub salt into the wound, writing furniture was probably introduced from France!

"It wasn't that we didn't write, we just didn't feel it necessary to write in style!"

Regency style
The table in question here is in rosewood and the top is veneered, although this would often have been lined with leather. Rather than having a leg at each corner, as in the earlier Chippendale period, it has end supports with platform bases, which was a popular Regency style of the early 19th century.

Problem
Apart from the usual worn drawer runners and bits of veneer that are making a bid for freedom or have escaped, there is a great deal of the moulding missing from the bottom edge of the frieze on this table.

The moulding is of the split, turned variety and, having measured the width and the thickness of the moulding, I established that it could not have been turned from a single piece of wood. Splitting the turning down the middle with a saw would have reduced the thickness – because

"Because of the thickness of the saw kerf, the turning must, therefore, be split without sawing!"

of the thickness of the saw kerf, the turning must, therefore, be split without sawing!

Preparation
Lengths of rosewood are prepared a little over-size – approximately the diameter of the turning in width and half the diameter in thickness – and two pieces were then stuck together to give the necessary size for turning.

ABOVE: The damage

ABOVE: The blank, with paper sandwiched between to allow for splitting later

BELOW: Making up the cutter for the moulding from an old spindle moulder blank

glue would be used for this, but PVA or Superglue can be used if you're in a hurry. Purists tend to go a little pale at the mention of the word Superglue when related in any way to antiques, but we're not using it to fix the moulding to the furniture so we should get away with it! If in doubt, don't tell anyone!

I am not a terribly brave man by nature, and don't like seeing bits of rosewood flying across the workshop when I'm turning – therefore the pieces are kept to a maximum length of about 200mm (8in). One end of the piece is held in a chuck as it is too small to be driven in any other way – the other end has to have a sharp point stuck right in the middle of the joint, which will tend to split the turning before you are ready. To overcome this the end is tightly bound with whipping twine, or something similar.

> "I am not a terribly brave man by nature, and don't like seeing bits of rosewood flying across the workshop when I'm turning"

However, if these two bits are just stuck together with glue that is 'stronger than the wood itself', it might be a bit of a challenge to get them apart when the turning is done! To get round this, a piece of paper is sandwiched between the two pieces when gluing. Traditionally, Scotch

Cutting bobbins

To make the cutting of the bobbins easy, quick and accurate, a cutter is made up out of a fairly thick piece of metal – in this case, an old spindle moulder cutter. Use a piece of Plasticine or dental moulding compound to transfer the profile from the original moulding to the cutter and use a combination of hacksaw and file to shape the metal. I find that a cutter that covers three bobbins works best.

Having made the cutter, turn a length of the jointed rosewood down to the finished diameter, then set out the bobbins with the cutter. At this stage just mark the position of the bobbins – which is made easy because the cutter covers three bobbins – and work from one end to the other, overlapping the cutter marks as you go.

A junior hacksaw is used next to deepen the cutter marks and some of the waste is then removed with the aid of a skew gouge, and a steady hand.

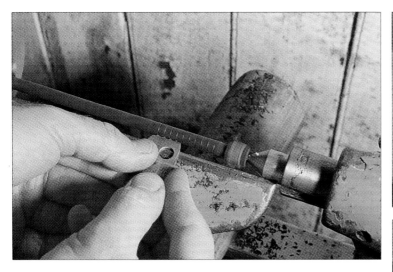

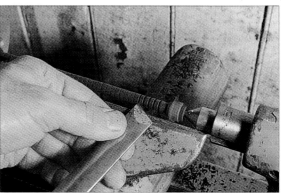

Final shaping

Final shaping is done with the cutter, which by now does not have too much wood to remove, and then, once again, the cutter is moved along, overlapping the previous cut each time.

Sanding and grain-raising is the last process, whilst still on the lathe and, having removed the whipping twine, the turning can hopefully be persuaded to split with the aid of a thin spatula.

> "Gluing the new moulding to the table would be easy if the missing bits were on the straight bits – but most of the missing bits are, of course, on the corners"

Steam bending

Gluing the new moulding to the table would be easy if the missing bits were on the straight bits – but most of the missing bits are, of course, on the corners and even though the mouldings are quite thin they cannot be persuaded to bend sufficiently without excessive assistance.

Steam bending is the answer for this little problem, and our high-tech steaming apparatus consists of a hot-plate with a metal bowl to hold the water and a piece of chipboard with a hole in the middle of it, sitting on top. The steam comes out of the hole in a nice jet and it is just a question of holding each piece of moulding in the steam until it becomes pliable without scalding your fingers.

The pieces are then strapped to some chipboard, which is cut to the same diameter as the table, with masking tape. Left overnight to set in its new shape, it is then fitted and glued to the table with Scotch glue. Masking tape can be used to

ABOVE LEFT: Initial marking with the cutter

TOP: Marks are deepened with a hacksaw

ABOVE: Skew chisel forms rough shape

LEFT: Moulding splits easily

PATINA

Patina is a word which is often used and often misunderstood in connection with items of antique furniture. The dictionary definition is 'encrustation, usually green, on surface of old bronze, esteemed as ornament; gloss produced by age on woodwork'.

Fairly obviously, a green encrustation on a piece of furniture is not in any way desirable but the 'gloss produced by age' and 'esteemed as ornament' is very relevant. This is still, however, rather vague and I believe that as far as furniture is concerned, patina is a combination of the oxidation of the wood and the 'gloss' produced by handling and waxing the furniture over a period of time.

The oxidation will change the colour of the wood to those familiar orangey-golden tones and the gloss comes from the grain being filled – these combine to give a real depth of colour and shine to the surface, and are both enhanced by the build-up of dirt in the mouldings and around the handles and other such places.

What patina is not, however, is the excessive build-up of dirt on the surfaces together with polish that has become tired and almost opaque, as can be seen on this table, particularly on the end supports and bases. When this has happened the beauty of the wood is to a large degree masked and, whilst I am not suggesting that Nitromorse should be slopped over fine pieces of furniture at will, there is often a case for sensitive and careful cleaning, and in some cases re-polishing, so that the wood can be seen again.

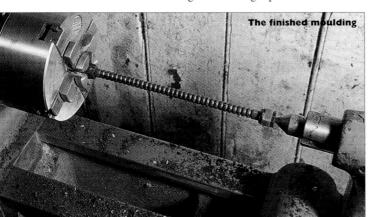

The finished moulding

ABOVE: High-tech steam bending

ABOVE: After steaming, the moulding is strapped around a former

hold the moulding while the glue hardens, but it is important to test whether the tape will remove any of the finish from the surrounding area – if it does, an alternative method of holding the moulding will be required.

As usual, a combination of chemical and cosmetic colouring systems are used to make it look as if the new pieces of moulding are meant to be there. ■

LEFT: Moulding is glued in place with Scotch glue

BELOW LEFT: Restored to former glory after polishing

EARLY DESIGNS

Early writing table designs included escritoires and bureaux, and later, pedestal desks – and although in the second half of the 18th century writing tables were made, they were mainly for libraries and were therefore also referred to as library tables. Often of a similar design to the sofa table, without the end flaps, some were also made round or multi-sided.

Frequently placed in the middle of a room, it meant that both sides of the table had to be useful and look pretty – the rectangular sort therefore had drawers on both sides, or at least real drawers on one side and dummy drawers on the other, while the round ones had drawers all the way round, often with alternate dummy fronts – just to make looking for your pencil more exciting!

Use and abuse

FURNITURE ABUSE — particularly to chests of drawers — is a misdemeanour to which most of us must own up.

A sudden whim to rearrange the furniture usually results in the chest being half lifted, half dragged fully loaded across the carpet. With a bit of luck all this ill-treatment will do is give the top a stress test and prove the strength of the bracket foot construction.

Drawers are also tested to destruction on a regular basis, being stuffed to bursting point.

Damage list

The chest I am working on is a George III specimen in solid mahogany with a serpentine front. Its feet are all sound, barring damage to the carved scrolls on the front ones.

The drawers have splits in their bottoms and the runners are worn, leading to a considerable amount of damage to the cockbeading; the carcass runners and drawer rails are also in need of help.

The top and one side of the chest both have bad splits which have been repaired in the past but have now opened up again!

As far as the finish is concerned, the top surface has over the years, thanks to granny's allegiance to hairspray, acquired a thick coating of lacquer, while the sides and feet have a considerable build up of dirt virtually obliterating the wood.

Standard repair

First to be attacked are the drawer and carcass runners.

That the runners require attention may be obvious because the top of the drawer front is tilting backwards or the drawer may just be difficult to open. A nasty screeching noise as the drawer is opened indicates that the veneer on the drawer rail has been loosened by the drawer running over its top edge, causing it to flap about.

MAIN SHOT: Split in side of carcass

BOTTOM RIGHT: Completed repair awaits staining

Another consequence of worn runners is damage to both cockbeading and drawer rails as they will inevitably start to hit each other; if the drawer stops have been foolishly fixed with nails the underside of the drawer bottoms will acquire a pair of neatly carved tram lines.

Runner wear

Drawer and carcass runners can both show wear. The drawers on this chest run on softwood dustboards which extend the full width and depth of the chest. The drawer rails are in solid mahogany.

"The top surface has over the years, thanks to granny's allegiance to hairspray, acquired a thick coating of lacquer"

The wear is seen as a trench in the softwood which continues across the mahogany rail, *see photo.* The serpentine shape results in a different problem in the fragile area where the rail meets the side of the chest; the friction from the drawer along with the wear to the top surface may result, as in this case, in a small piece falling off.

If the chest were not serpentine-fronted it is likely that the divider would be in softwood with a veneer on the front edge. Wear to the carcass will often loosen and ultimately damage the veneer.

Dustboard

The repair of the dustboard — filling the trench with new wood — is fairly straightforward.

Use the band saw to cut a piece of softwood to a width just a little greater than the width of the trench, with the grain running across the short dimension in the same direction as the grain in the dustboard.

Thickness this piece to a little more than the depth of the trench to allow for trimming flush when fitted, again using the band saw. Offer the piece up to its new home, holding it tight against the side of the chest.

Run a Japanese saw along the exposed edge of the repair piece, *see photo,* cut to about the same depth as the trench, remove the repair piece and cut again, but this time at the point where the dustboard meets the side of the chest.

Repeat this operation as often as is required for the length of the repair and simply butt each piece against its neighbour. The Japanese saw provides a crisp edge to the repair; because the blade is so fine the repair piece is still a snug fit .

Clean out the trench using a dog-leg or cranked chisel to produce a flat bottom, and Scotch-glue the repair piece into its new home. Cramping in this restricted space is made easy by using 'go bars' or a system of sticks and wedges, s*ee photo.*

Rail damage

Now for the slightly more demanding job of sorting out the damage to the mahogany drawer rail. The challenge is to remove as little of the original wood as possible while achieving a structurally sound repair which can be made to look as if it belongs.

To remove the damaged area, cut a long splice with a suitable, razor-sharp chisel. This splice will ensure the strength of the repair.

The piece of mahogany used to make the repair must have a grain as similar as possible to the original to increase the chances of ensuring that the glue line disappears. Having found the ideal piece, hand craft it to the required shape, remembering to orientate the grain in the repair to the grain in the rail!

The repair to the bottom carcass runner, where there was wear from the drawer, requires a double splice to reduce the amount of original wood removed, as does the repair necessitated by the missing piece.

Drawer runners

The drawers are all fairly sound, the runners merely becoming thinner towards the back, *see photo.* Building up the runners to their original thickness may be approached in one of two ways.

If the drawer is sound, dismantling it is unnecessary and will probably cause additional damage; therefore, with the drawer still in one piece, fit either a tapered piece to counteract the taper caused by wear, or — my preference — eliminate the taper and add a new piece of uniform thickness.

RIGHT: Completed repair or dustboard and front rail

ABOVE: Wear is seen as a trench in the softwood which continues across the mahogany rail; friction from the drawer, coupled with top surface wear, can result in a small piece falling off

ABOVE: Running a Japanese saw along exposed edge of the repair piece

ABOVE: 'Go bars' or sticks and wedges make cramping in a restricted place easy

ABOVE: **Bottom runner of drawer showing tapered wear**

ABOVE: **MDF jig and router set-up to clean off taper**

"A good way of cramping this repair is to use old upholstery springs which have been cut down to make spring cramps"

Either way, a router will be required.

To remove the taper place the drawer upside down on the bench and restrain it. Now find a piece of MDF which is a little longer than the runner and wide enough to give a stable platform on which the router can run.

Sit the MDF on the underside of the drawer bottom parallel and adjacent to the runner. Folding a couple of smallish pieces of garnet paper into three with the abrasive side facing out, slipping them between the drawer bottom and the MDF, stops any sliding around.

This technique not only provides a platform for the router, but will automatically trim the runner parallel to the drawer bottom — that's the theory anyway!.

Set the router's depth stop to the point where the runner is worn to its thinnest, don safety equipment and remove the taper, *see photo*.

Now make up a new piece to a suitable thickness, allowing 2 to 3mm ($^5/_{64}$ to $^1/_8$ in) for trimming, and glue to what is left of the original runner.

A good way of cramping this repair is to use old upholstery springs which have been cut down to make spring cramps. Protect the top edge of the drawer side while cramping with a piece of MDF/ply.

Finishing

Having let the glue go off, the repairs can be trimmed, care being taken not to take off any of the original surfaces! ∎

ABOVE: **Damage to underside of drawer front**
BELOW: **Spliced repair to underside of drawer front**

ABOVE: **Upholstery springs used as clamps for new piece of drawer runner**

On the edge

THE STYLE boys of the late 17th and early 18th century had a wonderful time developing the design and construction of drawers.

Initially, geometric mouldings glued and pinned to the fronts were the height of fashion, then later veneered drawer fronts became the standard with the addition of cross- and feather-banding. The mouldings were at this time relegated to the carcass and of a 'D' or double 'D' section.

Around 1710 a lip moulding was introduced which projected beyond the drawer on all sides and was half-round in section. Initially this took the form of a walnut strip which over-sailed the edges. This construction continued into the mahogany period and was around until about 1750.

However, thin bits of wood hanging off the edges of drawers are prone to damage, especially when the drawer stops fail and the lipping becomes a surrogate stop.

Fragility

Perhaps this inherent fragility had something to do with the next development, circa 1730 — the introduction of the cockbead on walnut and mahogany furniture.

While a cockbead is less likely to become damaged than a lip moulding, anything that sticks out a bit and is around the edge of something that moves and is handled by humans will suffer at some stage in its life.

When a chest of drawers fitted with cockbeading comes into the workshop, the chances are that it will require some attention; impact damage may have caused a dent or loosened the beading, causing it to flap about or to escape. Worn drawer runners also mean damage, especially to the bottom edge, as they cause the beading to catch on the drawer rail.

While not a structural problem, damaged or missing pieces of beading constitute an eyesore, but repairs are straightforward. The bow-fronted nature of the drawer illustrated adds a little to the challenge, but the theory is the same.

Japanese saw

Firstly, cut out the damaged section with a fine saw such as the Japanese type, but not too enthusiastically as even a fine saw cut in a drawer front is embarrassing. Using a saw rather than a chisel avoids breaking away the unsupported edge and extending the damage further.

The cut is made at an angle, never straight across the grain, for two reasons: firstly, the repair will be stronger; secondly, it is much easier to make an angled join 'disappear'.

Having found a suitable piece of wood, cut a piece that is generously oversized in its width and a little in its thickness, and transfer the angles of the cuts from the drawer using a piece of tracing paper; mark the grain

GENTLE TOUCH

WHEN TRIMMING and shaping the repair use the fingertips to run over the repair and the surrounding area, picking up lumps, bumps and imperfections in curves that the eye cannot see until the polish has been applied; light has a habit of showing up any faults like a beacon.

> "Anything that sticks out a bit and is around the edge of something that moves and is handled by humans will suffer at some stage in its life"

ABOVE: Unsightly damage to cockbeading on underside of drawer — the victim of an earlier, poor repair

direction on the tracing paper also as this must match.

Shooting board

Cut the angles of the repair piece with a saw and make fine adjustments with a block plane. A small shooting board provides a useful means of maintaining both control and a perpendicular cut — not to mention your fingertips!

When the piece fits between the angled cuts, trim its width and round off the inner edge to match the existing beading. Doing this before gluing avoids damaging the drawer front later. Glue with Scotch (hide) glue and, if necessary, hold the repair in place with veneer pins, pre-drilling first to avoid splitting. Avoid the temptation to punch the pins in and leave enough protruding so that they may be easily removed when the glue has set.

When dry, remove any pins and trim the top surface level without removing any of the adjacent original surface, *see panel*, then round over the outer edge.

Now all that remains is to blend the repair by damaging it to some degree — a process which goes against the grain after hours spent trying to achieve perfection. Blending is completed using chemical and cosmetic colouring systems. ▨

ABOVE: Repair in place — note the angled cut to provide strength and help the repair to disappear

ABOVE: Invisible mending — the repair is blended into the surrounding area and polished

A 'square' piano fully repaired

Fortification of

One of the joys of being a furniture restorer is the amount of interesting and varied pieces of furniture that come through the workshop. For some strange reason I have always had a soft spot for musical instruments, which may be due to their novelty value or their wonderfully intricate mechanisms; it certainly isn't because of my ability to play them!

Apart from musical boxes, the instruments that a furniture restorer is likely to be presented with are of the keyboard variety. Whilst we are all familiar with the modern upright and grand piano, I used to feel a bit confused when confronted with the antique variety if its correct name was demanded by its owner. Requests for this sort of information by a potential client may be

nothing more than an innocent quest for knowledge – it may on the other hand be a restorer credibility check, so a little research is useful both to broaden the mind and increase the chance of securing a commission.

Keyboard instruments

The first stringed instruments fitted with a keyboard had rectangular cases and were made in the 13th century, but were very rare in England. I understand that only one example exists in this country, so I have made the executive decision to never call whatever confronts me a 'clavichord'. We have all heard of virginals, spinets and harpsichords but are not necessarily aware of their differences. In fact, they all have one thing in common – the mechanism

plucks the strings as opposed to the modern piano which hits them with hammers.

The first of these to appear in the 14th century was the virginal; in common with the clavichord it had a rectangular case and was given the name because it was very popular in convents and with ladies. Apparently Henry VIII had a collection of more than 30 virginals by the time he died, which presumably says something about him, but I don't feel it appropriate that I should speculate on the subject in a woodworking magazine.

The 15th century saw the introduction of the harpsichord, which was shaped like a harp that had fallen over – rather similar to the modern-day grand piano; the end of this century saw the spinetta which came from Italy. The spinet, as we

V-blocks and large oak block set up to create flat faces for splicing in new wood

Routing more square faces to complete the repair

Splices in place prior to re-cutting thread

Depth having been established with a saw, the new thread is cut

a pianoforte

call it, came in various shapes, but to keep things simple I remember them as having that rather pleasing wing-shape.

Pianoforte

In about 1750 the pianoforte was invented – the name 'piano e forte' meaning soft and loud, a feature that could be achieved because the strings were struck with hammers, the volume being controlled by the players' degree of heavy handedness. Virginals and the like,

with their plucking mechanism, had no volume control!

The first incarnation of the pianoforte was known as the 'square piano' and must have been named by a rather misguided chap as they are in fact rectangular; uprights and grand pianos made their appearance in about 1860.

Square piano

So, taking all the above into account, I am able to deduce that the instrument I

have in my workshop is a square piano. I happen to know that this particular one was made by Muzio Clementi and his boys in London, and I know this because there is a label on it which says as much, and it was made early in the 19th century.

There are various types of furniture that have had their usefulness 'enhanced' by a little – or not so little – modification; night-tables or 'commodes' often have their pot holders turned into drawers and square pianos have their innards ripped out to transform them into drinks cabinets! Happily, though, this particular Clementi still had all its bits, although some of the bits, like the legs, were a bit frail and had became a matter of some concern to its owners. This worry of collapse was ➤

"Requests for this sort of information by a potential client may be nothing more than an innocent quest for knowledge – it may on the other hand be a restorer credibility check"

Finished repair

This leg required a complete new thread – a block is turned with a spigot to fit into the leg

Tape is put around a blank – the width of the pitch and cutting lines is marked on

The marked-out thread

➤ highlighted due to the arrival of a small but increasingly mobile person in their household who was convinced the piano was a Georgian climbing-frame.

Repairs

Square pianos are made in two bits – the musical bit which is just like a large but rather heavy rectangular box, and a stand to hold it at a convenient playing height. To make the whole thing more portable the legs are screwed into the stand and are removable, but these threaded wooden joints often get damaged. This usually results in a display of desperate measures to hold everything together – these legs didn't have many screws and nails but they did have more than their fair share of glue and car-body filler.

Once I had removed all the legs and cleaned them up it was obvious that it was almost exclusively the male part of the joint that was damaged, which is something that I have found is often the case. On all the legs I merely cleaned the residue of filler etc. from the female part

of the joint, as these threads were almost entirely intact.

Screw box

Wooden screw threads were traditionally cut using a screw box and a tap, and if you have the urge to cut wooden screw threads it is still possible to buy the tools. Nowadays they often come from Taiwan, but the thread on the ones I have come across seem to be quite fine; certainly not appropriate for cutting threads on antique furniture. I have occasionally seen old screw boxes in second-hand tool shops but I have never snapped one up, and the chances are that if I had it wouldn't be quite the right size for any restoration job that ever came my way.

Re-cutting

Without a nicely matching screwbox I was therefore faced with the prospect of repairing and re-cutting all the threads by hand – some of the threads just had sections missing while others had no thread remaining at all.

I tackled the threads with damaged sections first and these obviously needed to have any missing wood replaced. This could, I am sure, have been done by hand but as there were several to do I made the decision to use a router to create flat areas to splice onto. I made a pair of cradles with V-shaped cuts in to support each leg, and planed a couple of flat faces on a large lump of oak to sit the router on. The addition of a fence and a few cramps completed the arrangement which looked a little precarious, but worked well in practice.

Having routed a flat face to the damaged area, a piece of square section 'thread' was glued on and this process was repeated to cover all areas of damage. With the legs that had part of their threads remaining it was just a question of trimming the repair pieces to the outside diameter of the thread and then extending the line of the thread around with a pencil line. The valley of the thread was then cut in with a saw and the unwanted bits removed with a chisel.

Tape is used as a depth guide for initial cutting of new thread

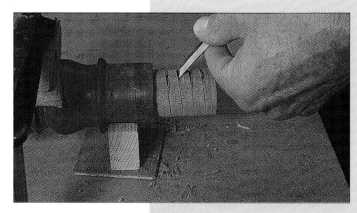

The thread is carefully cut with a chisel

"The first incarnation of the pianoforte was known as the 'square piano' and must have been named by a rather misguided chap as they are in fact rectangular"

A little fitting, adjusting and sanding creates a perfect fit

The legs with no thread at all or with the threaded section broken off needed rather more extensive surgery. This involved turning up a piece of mahogany to the outside diameter of the screw thread on the lathe, with a nice chunky spigot of a smaller diameter on the end to insert into the end of the leg. It may seem obvious, but it's a good idea to turn the spigot to the diameter of one of your drills!

Thread-marking

In previous issues I have mentioned the benefit of having a grey-haired, bearded restorer wearing half-rimmed specs in the workshop to enhance the workshop's credibility. I have also found it very useful on occasion to have an engineer in the workshop as they have brains that don't go like porridge when faced with working out things such as screw threads. They are also able to say things like 'pitch' and 'single start thread' whilst giving an air of knowing what they are talking about. Fortunately I have just such an engineer in my workshop who

also doubles as the chap with the half rim specs, which saves space!

So to lay out the thread with no original thread remaining, I measured the pitch of the female part of the thread – the distance between two peaks – and transferred this measurement to a piece of paper. I then cut out a parallel strip of paper of this width and of sufficient length to be wrapped around the entire length of a thread. In wrapping the strip of paper around at such an angle that the edges butt against each other, it will automatically set itself at the correct angle for the thread – obvious really!

Fitting

Having wrapped the strip around, I marked the thread by running a pencil round where the edges of the strip butted against each other; this line gave the position of the peaks. I then removed the strip and marked another line which I drew freehand at the mid point of the first line – this gave the position of the troughs. I then set in the troughs with a saw with the required depth of cut

marked on the saw blade with a piece of masking tape – the new thread was completed with a bit of chiselling, a bit of sanding, and quite a bit of trial and error in its new home to get the final fit right.

At the outset I thought this job could be a bit of a challenge but with my new-found thread-marking technology, some sharp chisels and some sandpaper it all went remarkably smoothly. I found that it was helpful to remember that the fit of these screw threads does not have to be too exact; I'm not suggesting that it is acceptable that they flap about, but when they are tightened they are able to take up a small amount of slack to become remarkably rigid.

Play or playing?

Despite all this repair work, I fear that the small person who shares his home with this instrument will still have to be persuaded that square pianos are not designed to be an aid to the development of motor skills. However, anyone actually playing it should not be distracted by the thought of crushed toes! ■

Sofa, so good

There seems to be some confusion amongst the antique furniture owning public as to the purpose of a sofa table. It has the word 'sofa' in its name so is it reasonable to assume it should have at least a tenuous link to a sofa? Well, you certainly wouldn't want to put it in front of your sofa because not only would it impede your view of the television but it would also make it very difficult to gain access to the coffee table. The dimensions of a sofa table make it far too long to put at the side of a sofa; so the only places that remain are, in the general vicinity of a sofa and behind the sofa. And behind the sofa is what it was obviously tailor made for, making it ideally suited for the display of little silver trinkets and photos of granny, perfectly placed behind your head so that you could admire your treasures at your leisure whilst relaxing on your sofa! Of course, it doesn't really matter where you put your sofa table but it was actually intended for use in

front of the sofa. Mr Sheraton commented, "ladies chiefly occupy them to draw, write or read upon." But ladies don't seem to want to indulge in these eminently worthy pastimes anymore, at least not whilst languishing on their sofa; so the sofa table nowadays usually finds itself behind the sofa in trinket display mode or just loitering about somewhere else...

A brief history

The sofa table was a development of the Pembroke table; it was introduced in circa 1790 and it gradually superseded the Pembroke, becoming very popular by the end of the 18th century. In many ways, the sofa table was similar to the Pembroke: both tables have short flaps

raised and supported on 'fly brackets' to enlarge the surface of the table. But the most obvious difference is the Pembroke has its flaps fitted to the long sides whereas a sofa table's flaps are fitted on its short sides.

Sheraton suggests they were generally made between 5 and 6ft long and from 22in to 2ft broad and there were two distinct types. The earliest design had vertical supports at each end – or 'end standards' – and, the earlier ones did not have a stretcher joining the end standards whereas the later ones did. The stretcher, if fitted, was generally turned and often carved as well.

The final variation had a central pedestal which consisted of anything from one to four columns which were

"There seems to be some confusion amongst the antique furniture owning public as to the purpose of a sofa table"

Routed out new socket for turned columns

MDF jig used with guide bush to rout out sockets

"Using a chisel and a mallet can be a little traumatic for antique components"

➤ usually turned. These sat on a flat rectangular base fitted with feet/legs at each corner. Another variation on this general theme I have come across had no end flaps but was fitted with extending pieces which could be drawn out from the ends. Some tables, too, were fitted with a chess board that was hidden beneath the top.

Pedestal

It is an example of the pedestal type I have been recently working on. The table is made in mahogany *(Swietenia sp)* with rosewood *(Dalbergia sp)* bandings and has a one or two gilt embellishments. The most exotic sofa tables were made in Macassar ebony *(Diospyrus macassar)*, also known as calamander in the antiques trade; zebrawood or zebrano *(Diospyrus microberlinia)*; rosewood and the like. So being made in mahogany doesn't make this the trendiest of sofa tables but, nevertheless, it is nicely made. The top is in solid mahogany with a rosewood banding let in. There is a

frieze drawer on one side which has no visible handle; instead the drawer rail is scalloped away to allow fingers to get behind the bottom edge of the drawer front, the drawer is fitted with quadrant drawer slips which gives a pointer to its being later Regency. The only decoration to the frieze is a split turned quadrant moulding which runs around the inside edges of the panels and there is a gilt honeysuckle *(anthemion)* decoration in the middle of the drawer and dummy drawer fronts.

The two turned columns have a lovely shape and they sit on a veneered base which has very restrained ebony line inlay which is repeated on the very 'Regency' legs with their knobbly knees. The legs terminate in gilt lion's paw feet and castors, although sadly most of the gilding has long since departed. The only other decoration is in the form of gilt Tudor roses fitted to the tops of the legs on either side of the knees. Another little detail I came across was two small pegs fitted to the frame of the table at each end which are positioned to act as a

stops for the leaves when they are in the down position. These ensure the leaves rest in the vertical position; anything other than a vertical dangle can look sloppy.

A final touch that caught my eye was the 'fly brackets' which support the leaves when up. These have well shaped ends instead of the rather uninspired 'blobby' things that are often to be found. They are much darker than the frieze but this is because they've been hiding under the flaps for most of their lives and, consequently, their colour has not changed in the same way as the rest of the table exposed to the light.

Table top

There were two main structural areas on this table requiring attention: the top which was flapping about rather alarmingly at its joint with the turned columns and a couple of the legs were losing their grip on the base.

To do anything useful to the wobbly top I first had to dismantle it which was not too difficult as it just involved

'New' wood in place

Socket cut on morticer for replacement of dovetail on the leg/base joint

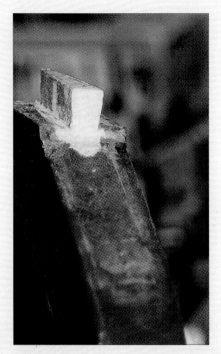

New dovetail

Dovetail socket in base

extracting some screws. Having done this it became obvious the flapping had been going on for some considerable time, as the circular holes in the bearer that the columns were fitted into were a great deal less circular than they had once been. Even though there was considerable movement in the joints, it was not possible to actually remove the bearer from the tops of the columns without removing the wedges fitted to the tops of the columns to expand them into the holes for a nice tight fit. There is, unfortunately, no magical method I know of to remove these wedges and they always put up a fight but a concerted effort with some small chisels and a large mallet will always get you there in the end.

In some cases, with this 'wobbly top' problem, you can get away with packing the joint but this one was a too far gone, so I decided the sensible thing to do would be to make the holes round again! To achieve this I made up an MDF template and, with the use of a router fitted with a guide bush, I routed away a section of wood around the areas with the worst wear. Having squared up the internal corners I was able to drop in a new piece of beech *(Fagus sp)* which I was able to trim to form a nice round hole again. I then glued the bearer back onto the columns with some pearl glue and fitted some new wedges. You must have the wedges ready for this bit because it's no good gluing the bearer on and then running off to make wedges while the glue is setting, it must be done in one operation if success is high on your list of priorities.

Leg base joints

The other major structural problems were the leg base joints: one was obviously very fragile and another was loose but a complete collapse was being prevented because metal reinforcing brackets had been added. Having removed the brackets, the worst leg fell off and the other just wobbled a bit ➤

Complete repair

"Apart from these repairs and a few minor veneer repairs, the only other area that required attention was at the ends of the frieze; the problem here was really an inherent design weakness"

After Mr Lloyd has worked his magic

➤ more. These joints usually consist of a stopped sliding or slot dovetail and in this case they were tapered. In modern furniture this opportunity to show a little craftsmanship would be substituted with a few dowels – very creatively fulfiling!

The leg that had fallen off had done so because the dovetail was no longer attached and its housing in the base was fine, apart from the fact that it had a dovetail stuck in it. To recreate the dovetail I put the leg into the morticer and cut a fairly deep mortice. Not every furniture restorer will have a morticer but when creating false tenons – or sliding dovetails – they are often a very good option because they are nice and gentle. Using a chisel and a mallet can be a little traumatic for antique components!

I cut the mortice so it was at right angles to the leg's shoulder and the new piece of wood that I glued into it had its grain running parallel to the mortice. Now this is not strictly correct if you want the new dovetail to be a replica of

the original because the original dovetail was obviously cut from the lump of wood that made up the leg. This would have meant that the grain in the dovetail would have been running at an angle to the shoulder to give the leg its overall strength. The new dovetail will, therefore, be a little stronger than the original. It doesn't make a huge difference but every little helps – not to mention the fact that it also makes the execution of the repair slightly easier!

Having fitted the new lump of wood into the mortice, all that remained was to fashion it into a shape that would fit snugly in its housing. To achieve this I marked out its general shape with a pencil and then refined the shape by using a good deal of trial and error having previously removed the original dovetail from the housing!

The other leg, which was just wobbling a bit, I removed from its housing and spliced its dovetail at one end where a bit had fallen off. Having done this and cleaned the housing, I re-glued it which gave a nice solid result.

Frieze

Apart from these repairs and a few minor veneer repairs, the only other area that required attention was at the ends of the frieze; the problem here was really an inherent design weakness. The vertical pieces of mahogany at the ends of the frieze were fitted directly over the knuckle joints of the fly brackets, this meant that a proportion of the wood that was directly under the mahogany moved every time the fly brackets were moved. All I could do here was to ensure there was a little clearance between the moving part and the mahogany and re-glue the loose pieces, ensuring the glue only found its way onto the bits that weren't meant to move. Glue everywhere would possibly have made a stronger joint but fly brackets with fixed knuckle joints are not particularly useful. The only other thing I did was to tell the table's owner if he were too dynamic in his approach to fly bracket twiddling he would ultimately have to bring his table to see me again. He hasn't been back yet! ■

Almost a copy...

RECENTLY I WAS speaking to another furniture restorer, and we both agreed that a lot of restorers are frustrated makers. We also agreed that the things we liked making most were chairs; they are usually something of a challenge and so satisfying to make.

My approach to making or copying furniture has always been to say: "yes, of course I can…" and worry about how to actually do it on the way home in the car – and sometimes for a considerable time afterwards!

Near copy

The chairs shown here are relatively straightforward, apart from their backs which have curves going in a rather worrying number of different directions.

At times like this, the only way I have found that concentrates my mind in a productive manner, is to retreat to my drawing board and draw everything full-size.

From a full size drawing, joints may be worked out and templates made up

for any complicated components; in fact, by the time I had finished these chairs I had more than a dozen templates and drawings for their various elements.

The original that I was to copy was in my possession, so the drawings were straightforward but for the fact that the original has arms and the chairs I was making do not – and therefore have a smaller seat.

This meant that only the height of the seat and cresting rails could be taken from the original, other dimensions being scaled down. My client opted for stuff-over seats of the same thickness as the squab cushions on the cane-seated original.

Curves

My first drawing was not full-size, as its purpose was to get the look of the whole chair right in this narrower form, especially the curves of the back. Having achieved this, the various elements of the chair may be drawn up full-size, with details such as size and depth of mortice and tenon joints – and importantly, their angles relative to their shoulders.

From these drawings the thickness of timber that will be required in order to achieve the various curved elements of the chair can be calculated – each slender, curved piece forming the splat, for example, requires a piece of wood with an overall cross-section of 114 by 86mm (4½ by 3⅜in).

"Only the height of the seat and cresting rails could be taken from the original, other dimensions being scaled down"

"The sort of thing your woodwork teacher trotted out as you tried to hide yet another piece of decimated rainforest up your jumper"

ALL PICTURES ON THIS PAGE:
Some interesting compound curves are to be found in the splat and crest rail, requiring thick stock and careful drawing

"Pigeon-toed chairs are not a design feature I want to be remembered for!"

Machining

Having taken delivery of the necessary Brazilian mahogany (*Swietania macrophylla*) and beech (*Fagus sylvatica*), some of which was in frighteningly muscle-building sections, I wished, yet again, that I had a bigger workshop and a crosscut saw!

Once the timber was converted into slightly more manageable chunks – with a combination of Skilsaw and panel saw – it was machined up for the various components of the chairs.

Because there were six of each to be made, each part could be processed as a batch, thereby saving time by only having to set machines up once.

This method also has the potential of repeating a wrong setting many times, and gives greater meaning to that rather annoying saying: "measure twice and cut once" which is the sort of thing your woodwork teacher trotted out as you tried to hide yet another piece of decimated rainforest up your jumper.

Front legs

The legs are a fairly important (!) part of a chair, and are therefore a good place to start. The front legs are turned and require a template for the profile; this makes it easy to take measurements with callipers, is much more convenient than balancing the chair you are copying on the end of the lathe, and prevents damaging the original leg during repeated measuring.

The mortices are cut while the legs are still square.

The only tricky bit of these turnings, apart from having to make twelve legs look the same, is in the forming of a splay at the foot. This is achieved by first profiling the concave part of the splay on the lathe then, having raised the grain and sanded whilst still on the lathe, the legs are cut to their finished length and the rest of the splay formed with a bandsaw and a spokeshave.

The only guidance I can offer here is, having cut the leg to its final length, use a template to draw a circle on the end of the leg. This will be its footprint, and gives a good guide for shaping. It is important to ensure that the toe is pointing in the right direction in relation to the mortices, pigeon-toed chairs are not a design feature I want to be remembered for!

Back legs

The profile of the back legs is transferred using a thin plywood template; this template also has holes for transferring the positions of the mortices for the rear seat rail, and the

rail that supports the splat.

The position of the side rails' mortices may also be transferred from this template, although a mortice gauge is needed to mark their width.

By the time the legs arrive at the morticer their backs, having been bandsawn, are concave and therefore require the support of a softwood former, its function being not only to support the leg, but to

offer it up so that the mortices are cut at the correct angle.

Making a mark on the former which can be aligned with another on the legs ensures that the same angle results for every leg. ∎

Copies complete

IN THIS, the second of my two part article we look at the rails, jointing and splats - and finally complete the set of chairs!

Seat

Beech is used for the seat rails because the seats are to be upholstered, and beech does not split when tacks are put into it. To achieve the same look as the original chairs, the lower 42mm (1⅝in) of the rails is veneered with mahogany, at a later stage. The front and back rails are straight in their length, and curved in their depth, to give a dish to the seat – the side rails are the reverse.

Cutting tenons

To make the cutting of the tenons quicker, the front and back rails are first machined to their overall dimensions, and the tenons cut before the rails are shaped. It is important when machining up a batch of components, to cut each set to exactly the same dimensions, and clearly mark the face-sides and face edges.

I cut the shoulders of the tenons on the table saw using a sliding carriage. A stop is set on the fence of this so that a cut to each end of the rail results in the required dimension between the shoulders. The only other consideration is the depth of cut which varies, depending on which face is being cut. This is where the orientation of the face side and edge marks is critical, as a moment's loss of concentration could result in some colourful language, and what was a harmless seat rail becoming a dangerous projectile – at least, that is the effect it has on me!

The cheeks of the tenons are cut on the bandsaw after which the rails are shaped, again on the bandsaw.

Side rails

The same approach could be taken for the side rails but would waste a huge amount of wood, therefore the stock is machined to thickness and the profile marked out from a template. The curves can be marked out in pencil, but the shoulders and tenons should be knifed for accuracy. The rails are then cut to profile and the bulk of the waste around the tenons removed on the bandsaw. The scribed line for the shoulders is extended around each end and final shaping of the shoulders and cheeks is done by hand, with a chisel.

"A moment's loss of concentration could result in some colourful language, and what was a harmless seat rail becoming a dangerous projectile!"

RIGHT: John Lloyd's armless copy

> "One thing to remember is that these pieces are handed – twelve identical pieces will not have the right effect at all!"

ABOVE LEFT: Knife the shoulders of the side seat rails before...

ABOVE: ...cutting them back with a chisel

Cresting rail

The cresting rail is a bit of a challenge in that the mortices are at different angles – this is overcome by, once again, cutting the mortices while the rail is still square. The profiles and positions of the mortices are marked out from templates, and pairs of softwood wedges are made up with angles which correspond to those of the mortices. Each rail is then positioned in the morticer with the appropriate pair of wedges while each mortice is cut.

This system ensures that the mortice angles of all the cresting rails are the same – they may all be wrong but they will certainly be the same!

Profiling

Once the mortices are cut, the rest of the profiling can be done on the bandsaw, but the sequence of which face is cut first must be given some thought so that there is always a flat face available to bear on the table.

The double curve of the pieces forming the splat is approached in a similar way to a cabriole leg, the only difference being that a cabriole is symmetrical and the splat is not. A cabriole, therefore, requires one template and the splat requires two to reflect the different curves in the two elevations, the templates being taken from the full scale drawings of the front and side views.

Cutting

The overall size of the pieces required for these parts is measured accurately from the drawings and, while the wood is still square, the positions of the shoulders of the tenons are scribed top and bottom.

The curves are drawn from the templates on two adjacent faces using the scribed shoulder lines for positioning. One thing to remember is that these pieces are handed left and right – twelve

BELOW: Note that the angles of the tenons of back legs and splat are different

> "This system ensures that the mortice angles of all the cresting rails are the same – they may all be wrong, but they will certainly be the same!"

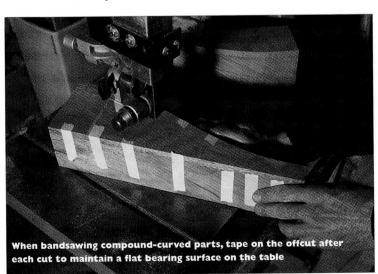

When bandsawing compound-curved parts, tape on the offcut after each cut to maintain a flat bearing surface on the table

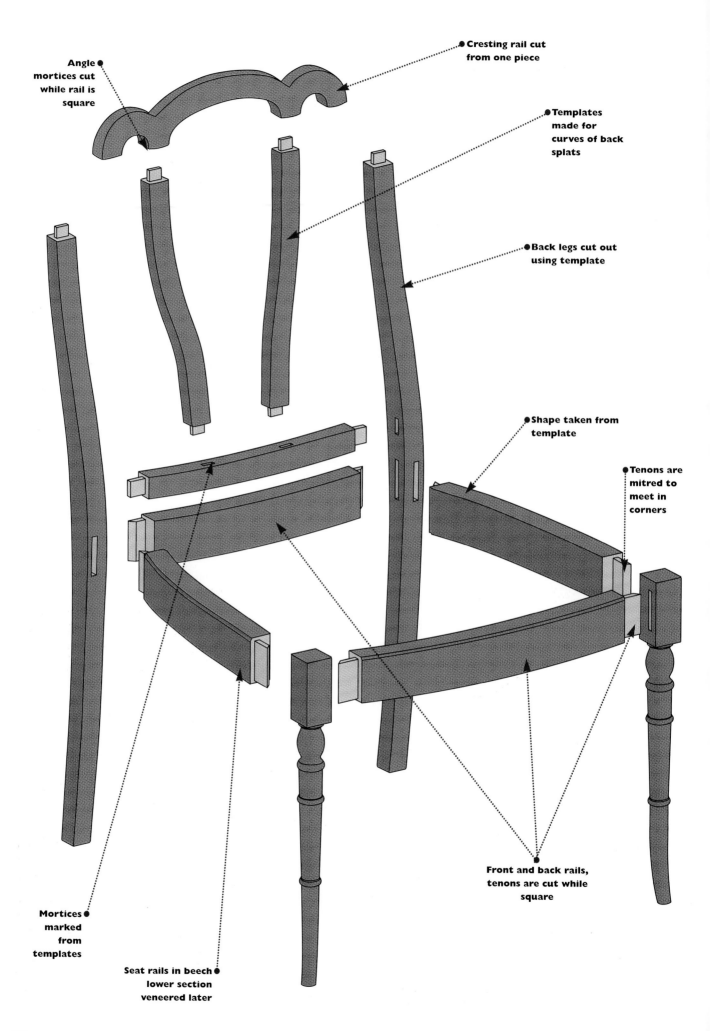

Angle mortices cut while rail is square

Cresting rail cut from one piece

Templates made for curves of back splats

Back legs cut out using template

Shape taken from template

Tenons are mitred to meet in corners

Front and back rails, tenons are cut while square

Mortices marked from templates

Seat rails in beech lower section veneered later

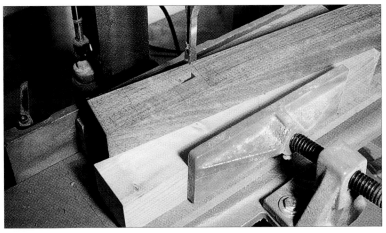

LEFT: Make wedges for angled morticing

LEFT AND BELOW LEFT: When bandsawing the crest rail give thought to the order in which each cut is made

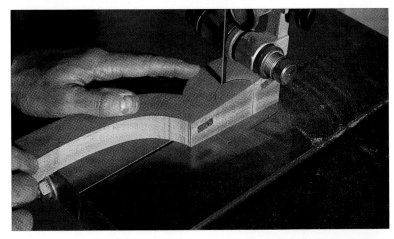

LEFT: Final shaping is done after gluing-up; first with a spokeshave and then with a cabinet scraper

identical pieces will not have the right effect at all!

Using the bandsaw, cut to the lines on one face, then tape the pieces back together with masking tape and cut to the lines on the other face. Leaving a short section square at each end gives a useful datum to work from when creating the tenons.

The tenons are marked out using the scribed shoulder lines and the short square sections as references. The measurements and angles are, once again, taken from the drawings – the angles being the same as the mortices on the cresting rail.

The only joints remaining to be cut are the tenons on the ends of the back legs, and these are done in the same way, remembering that the angle of the tenon is different.

Assembly

The backs are now assembled dry, joints are checked and adjusted if necessary, and the curve of the cresting rail is transferred to the tops of the back legs and the splat.

Having knocked the back apart again, the twists can be worked to each piece – this blends them from the square section just above the seat rails, to the curve of the cresting rail, but need not be done too accurately at this point. The final shaping of the various components which form the back is done when glued-up.

All the components should therefore be slightly oversize so that each piece may be blended into the next with nicely flowing curves, using a spokeshave for the rough shaping, and a cabinet-scraper to finish.

Veneer

When the chairs have been glued-up and the shaping completed, the pieces of veneer can be cut from the same mahogany as the rest of the chair and glued to the lower part of the seat rails.

Preparation for caning

The chairs are now complete, apart from the drilling of the holes in the backs for the caning. This is not just a question of copying the original layout, as the backs have been scaled down so, once again, this has to be drawn up full size until the

"Drilling the 1,200 holes for the six chairs has to be one of the most mind-numbingly tedious things you will ever have to do"

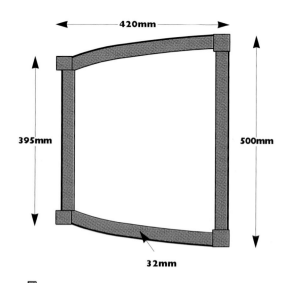

420mm

395mm

500mm

32mm

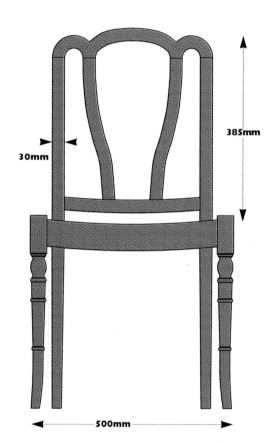

30mm

385mm

500mm

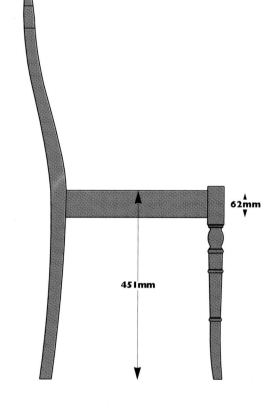

62mm

451mm

right spacing and overall effect is achieved.

More templates are required to transfer the positions of the holes to the chairs using a spike. Drilling the 1,200 holes for the six chairs has to be one of the most mind-numbingly tedious things you will ever have to do – it is a task that should, if at all possible, be delegated to someone you loathe.

Colouring

Colouring of the chairs to match the original is done with water stains, and the polishing done by hand with shellac. The chairs may then be sent away for caning and, on their return, the cane aged and the chairs waxed before being upholstered and delivered to a delighted client – you hope! ■

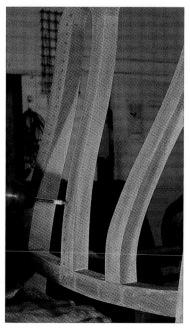

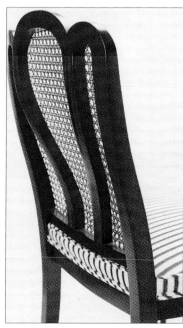

Tea-table trou

THERE is an inherent weakness in the leg-to-column joint in tripod tables. The joint itself is a dovetail housing with a sliding dovetail on the legs – but the legs have a natural tendency to splay outwards which puts a strain on the bottom of the column and the edges of the housings. On this particular specimen, even though these joints have been strengthened from beneath with a wrought iron bracket, the legs have managed to do the splits (literally) and need a little surgery.

Dismantling the joint is always the first requirement and, if the damage is extensive, it may fall apart – otherwise it is a question of introducing some warm water into the joint and applying some pressure in an appropriate spot. As with all dismantling, patience may be necessary while the old glue softens, to avoid further destruction.

Once apart, the joints are cleaned and, if water has been used, the old Scotch glue should be quite soft and easy to scrape off the surfaces – but if the joints were of the 'just fell apart in my hands' variety a little softening will be required. To do this in a painless way you need kitchen roll, cling-film and water.

ABOVE: Folding top allows the table to be stored away

Fold two to three sheets of kitchen roll to the required size to fit around the joint, wet the paper and wrap it around the joint, cover with cling-film, and go and drink tea or work on something else for a while. In about 20 minutes, depending on how thick the glue is, it becomes jelly-like and is easy to remove. Remember to label the legs and housings before starting the dismantling so that it is obvious which bit goes where when it comes to gluing-up. There aren't that many permutations for three legs and three housings but it is a good habit to get into when taking anything apart!

> "To make it easy to pinch someone else's cuppa when they weren't looking, the top could spin round if fitted with a bird-cage mechanism"

RIGHT: A popular piece of furniture in the 18th century – and the 20th!

bles brewing

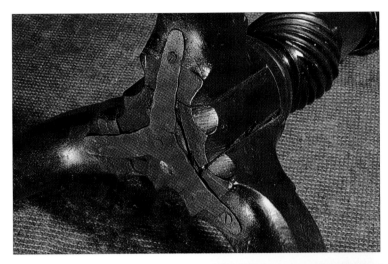

"There aren't that many permutations for three legs and three housings but it is a good habit to get into when taking anything apart!"

Split pillar

On this table, splits had developed along the pillar between the housings, and the front edge of one of the housings had broken out. The splits in the pillar couldn't be coaxed back together again so wood had to be introduced to fill the gaps and stabilise them. To give the repair a chance, the sides of the split were made clean and parallel using a junior hacksaw blade with the pin taken out of one end. For a wider split use two hacksaw blades at the same time, tape them together at one end and just run them down the split with a sawing motion. Create a fill-in piece from some of the right species of timber, glue-up and cramp.

The breakout from the edge of the housing needed a splice and the edge of one of the dovetails needed the same treatment, which was followed by a little whittling. Because the

TEA DRINKING NATION

We have been brewing tea in this country since the 17th century, thanks to the East India Company, and by the middle of the 18th century people were drinking it by the gallon. Initially tea was thought to have medicinal properties but later became simply fashionable and remained so until about 1750 when, as with all fashions, it very quickly became terribly naff. Tea drinking in public tea gardens was no longer the done thing, but it had become so much a way of life that it continued in private.

When tea drinking was done at home, something was needed to put all the cups, saucers and other tea-making paraphernalia on. There were, of course, tables designed for the taking of tea

at the end of the 17th century, but by the 18th century they were in short supply. The designers of the day got to work – and one of the tables that became popular, and is still found in some number today, is the round topped tripod tea-table. This design probably evolved from candlestands, which were of a similar design, but with a much smaller diameter top.

The top was hinged to allow the table to be placed against a wall to save space, this feature being known as a tip-up top or tilt top. It was often dished with a pie-crust edging and, to make it easy to pinch someone else's cuppa when they weren't looking, the top could spin round if fitted with a bird-cage mechanism.

ABOVE: Joint apart – the damage is apparent

splits in the column would not go back together, the housings were a little larger than they should be and some packing pieces were required to stop any movement in the joints when assembled.

Stabilising splits

There were two splits in the table's top which started at the edge and ran along the grain. They were straight and not very long, and were quite mobile and in need of stabilising.

A way of dealing with this is to insert dowels from the edge along the length of the split – because the hole/dowel is circular, and half the dowel is on each side of the split, it will restrain any lateral movement.

"The sight of a drill bit coming through the top surface of a table is not a pleasant one, and would be guaranteed to spoil your day, so a little thought and preparation is needed"

PIE-CRUST EDGING

The pie-crust edging had some serious damage which needed a splice. The position of the damage was fortunate in that there was no end-grain involved and the splice just meant levelling the bottom of the area of damage and squaring up the ends

with a chisel. I made the ends perpendicular, but not quite parallel, to give a slight taper and matched this taper on the repair piece to give a good snug fit. Gluing and cramping were followed by a little light carving to blend the repair in.

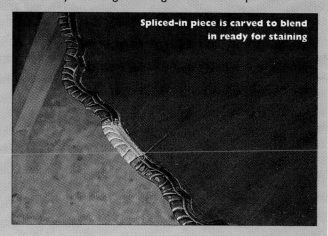

The damaged pie crust carving

Spliced-in piece is carved to blend in ready for staining

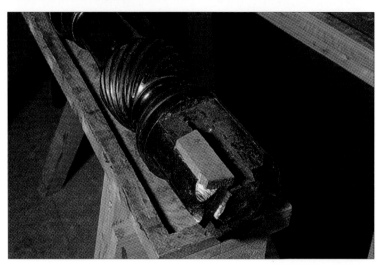

Mark the required depth of drilling on the drill bit with a piece of masking tape. The two sides of the split must be held so that the top surface is in register during drilling and gluing – this can be simply achieved with a couple of MDF offcuts and a cramp. Remember to put some greaseproof paper or similar between the MDF and the table surfaces as glue will often be forced through the split when the dowel is being introduced. The size of the hole/dowel is dictated by the thickness of the table and the dowel should be made from the same species of timber as the table, which inevitably means that home-made dowels are required. The timber used for dowels should be as straight-grained as possible – cut the wood to a square section and slightly oversize on the bandsaw, taper one end and take off the arrises with a block plane, keeping finger tips well away, and knock through a dowel plate of the required diameter.

All repairs are later blended using chemical and cosmetic colouring systems. ∎

LEFT: This dovetail needs some splicing and whittling as well

LEFT: Splices glued, the pillar is ready for re-shaping

> "The dowel should be made from the same species of timber as the table, which inevitably means that home-made dowels are required"

BELOW LEFT: The top restored to its original fine colour and finish

This may sound simple but before a dowel can be inserted, a hole must be created which generally involves drilling. The sight of a drill bit coming through the top surface of a table is not a pleasant one, and would be guaranteed to spoil your day, so a little thought and preparation is needed.

To be successful, this repair requires that the drilled hole runs as accurately as possible down the centre of the split – a piece of masking tape on the table's surface will make the line of the split more obvious, but to get lined up in the other direction a friend with a keen eye is needed! Alternatively, if no friends are to be found or trusted, drill a perpendicular hole in a suitably shaped piece of MDF with the pillar drill, cramp the MDF to the table's edge in the appropriate position and use the hole in the MDF to guide the drill perpendicular to the table's edge.

DOWEL PLATES

Dowel plates are easily made from a piece of 6mm (¼in) mild steel with holes drilled in it. Mine has holes of 0.5mm (⅟₆₄in) increments. Because the dowel is going into end-grain when it is trimmed, the end-grain of the dowel, together with a little colour, will make the repair invisible.

Doweling will ensure the split in the top goes no further

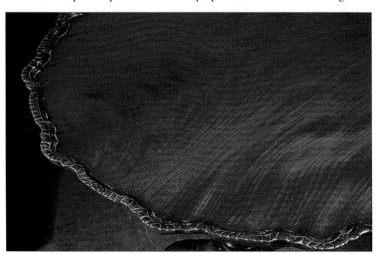

Restoring a lunch

RIGHT: Softwood blocks, made to match the curve of the back, support the laminations while gluing-up

BELOW RIGHT: Middle lamination glued over large area to give extra support

BOTTOM RIGHT: Final lamination glued in place

A RECENT VISITOR to the workshop was a mahogany Chippendale-style carver with a pierced splat. The cause of the damage, as described by my client, was the classic, rather large Sunday lunch guest, who had eaten far too much and consumed an enormous amount of liquid refreshment, which caused him to become rather exuberant whilst still within the confines of this fine chair. The end result was, as is always the case, the sound of splintering mahogany.

When examining the damage it quickly became obvious that the splat was made up of three laminates, which I had not come across before, but seemed a good way of strengthening a construction with obvious weak points. Apart from the area at the top, which had exploded, there were many other areas that were de-laminating, which pointed to the fact that perhaps it was failing glue which had created the weakness – the large guest's behaviour merely highlighting it.

Restorer's enemy

It also became obvious that this was not the first athletic lunch guest this chair had endured, as there were areas of the back covered in the restorers' enemy – when used in the wrong place

"When examining the damage it quickly became obvious that the splat was made up of three laminates, which I had not come across before"

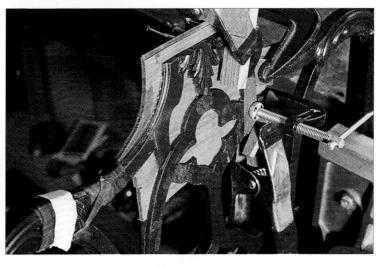

time drama

"This was not the first athletic lunch guest this chair had endured"

– epoxy resin! It was not just in the joints, but encasing them, and these areas were gaping and misaligned. The practice of repairing what are usually awkward breaks with epoxy resin, seems to me to be a result of either blind optimism, blind panic, or having been taken in completely by the latest advertising campaign!

Because the splat had been forced backwards, it was the laminates at the rear that had shattered most dramatically. This fact, combined with the epoxy factor resulted in the decision to sacrifice sections of the middle and rear laminates whilst preserving as much as possible of the original front laminate.

"The answer was to laminate the laminate"

The first process was to consolidate the areas of the splat which were just de-laminating. This involved cleaning the joint, where possible, introducing Scotch glue to it with a combination of a syringe and artists' spatula, and cramping-up using shaped softening blocks to match the curve of the splat.

Cresting rail

The cresting rail was then persuaded to part company from the rest of the chair whilst supporting the splat with a sandwich of shaped softwood formers. The splat was then once again supported, this time on only the front face, whilst the sections of the rear and middle laminates were removed – which was something of a challenge when some of the epoxy was still hanging on tight. Nitromors Craftsman was used to soften the epoxy where possible, but this is a long process and risked removing the original finish from the front face!

Middle laminate

The repair of the middle laminate had to be attempted next. It quickly became obvious that with the grain direction running across the curve of the back it was going to be impossible to effect the repair by just bending a single laminate to the curve as there

was far too much spring in it. The answer, therefore, was to laminate the laminate! The formers were made up from softwood and the three laminates thicknessed to give the required finished thickness – this was then glued up with the grain of all three laminates running in the same

ABOVE:
Chippendale-style chair, restored to its pre-lunch-guest beauty

ABOVE: Cutting out the shape before replacing the cresting rail

ABOVE: Reformed tenon – notice the three layers of laminations

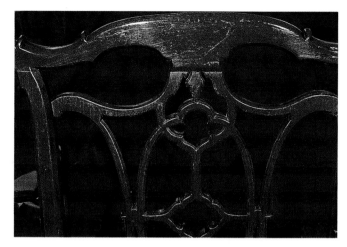

direction, using Cascamite to encourage the laminates to stay in the required shape. The curved laminate was then offered up to its new home, and scarf joints cut where the new laminate met the old, to avoid weak spots. The new laminate was then glued to the original front laminate, this time with Scotch glue, and an alarming number of cramps!

> "The new laminate was then glued to the original front laminate, this time with Scotch glue, and an alarming number of cramps!"

Rear laminate

The rear laminate was rather more straightforward as the grain was running in the right direction, vertically – and could therefore be encouraged into the required shape without the need for laminating it. So that strength was not compromised, the rear laminate was fitted with healthy overlaps to cover the middle laminate joints, and scarf joints were again used as necessary to avoid any weakness where end-grain meets end-grain.

Gluing-up was once again with Scotch glue and a worrying number of

> "The main assets in this kind of endeavour are razor sharp tools and your fingertips"

cramps. In both gluing operations strips of inner tube were stretched and tied around the scarf joints to give positive pressure to this area of the joint.

Stress tests

Having survived the cramp-induced stress tests, the next stage was to let in a couple of patches to the front face of the splat where the original breaks left untidy splintered joints; then the new

laminates and repairs were cut and shaped in an endeavour to make them look as if they belonged in their new home. During this operation the back needed support and this was achieved using a piece of MDF, a spacer block, and a few cramps – the splat would in this way get support from the back legs.

The important part of shaping any patch is to get the levels right, the old and new surfaces must flow into each other – in this case the surfaces were curved and pierced, which made life a little more of a challenge. The main assets in this kind of endeavour are razor sharp tools and your fingertips – constantly run your fingertips over the surfaces to detect those lumps and bumps that are not detectable with your eyes, in fact closing your eyes when doing this sometimes helps.

Cosmetics

The job was completed with the use of chemical and cosmetic colouring systems and polished to blend. The wood was sealed with shellac once the colour had been achieved, the surface was then built up, and the grain filled with wax. ■

To avoid the embarrassing addition of pieces of softwood or MDF glued firmly to a valuable piece of furniture, a piece of baking parchment is placed between the block and the part being glued!

When cabinets took silk

**Chiffonier with wired doors –
the height of fashion, according to Sheraton**

f you don't know the chiffonier as an item of antique furniture, the word may well conjure up images of the diaphanous material your mother or sister employed in the Fifties to encase their hairdresser's latest lacquer-enhanced triumph, to protect it from the ravages of an English summer.

The connection is 'chiffon' – that being the name of a material used to embellish ball-gowns and the like, as well as headscarves. If you are French, and the word is spelt with a double 'n' – 'chiffonnier' – you would be referring to a rag-and-bone man and 'chiffon' would mean a piece of rag. And the connection with pieces of fine furniture? – you'd think there should be some sort of link, however tenuous… Well, there is a link relating to fabric, although this may have no bearing on the way the antique came by its name, because the French described a chiffonier as, "a piece of furniture with drawers in which women put away their needlework".

Writing slide

So there you have it. A chiffonier (with one 'n') in France was a tall chest of drawers, made in some quantity from about 1750, for putting your bits of unfinished sewing in. But just when you thought you had it all sorted out, along comes the 'chiffonière', this being a small chest of drawers on legs which was sometimes fitted with a writing slide!

You may have started off feeling rather ambivalent about chiffoniers, but at this point you have probably developed a deep dislike of them and would rather you didn't ever hear of them again. I have to say that I do rather sympathise, but I'm afraid that I'm not going to give up, having got this far!

We now know what a chiffonier is in France, in all its various forms and spellings – which if nothing else may come in useful one day when playing Trivial Pursuit. But it is probably

"This is not a Victorian improvement but an example of a good quality Regency chiffonier"

ABOVE **Underside shows original inky tones of freshly worked rosewood**

The solid turned rosewood feet all needed re-gluing

LEFT **Solid rosewood supports show acanthus detailing, a classic Egyptian motif of the period**

"The shelf assembly on this piece was flapping about all over the place"

➤ more relevant to establish what the expression means in England.

Open shelves

Well the word came from France – surprise, surprise! – and was used in England from the end of the 18th century, when it tended to mean a cabinet with shelves or a cupboard and open shelves perched on top, the latter described by one George Smith in 1808 as being "chiefly for such books as are in constant use and not of sufficient consequence for the library".

So having just spent a great deal of time and effort establishing the derivation of the word chiffonier when used to describe a piece of French furniture, the term travels across a narrow strip of water and in the process mutates into a small bookcase which is suitable for housing the works of Delia Smith and Jilly Cooper!

Today the descriptive term chiffonier generally applies to the small bookcase version, this being a cabinet with an open shelf or shelves perched on top. The top shelf will almost certainly have a brass gallery running around three of its edges and the doors to the cabinet will often have a panel of brass latticework with silk lining behind.

Sheraton

The piece that I am working on this month has this general format and is of a style redolent of the Regency period. The veneer is rosewood and the brass fitments are gilt – which gives a pointer to its quality. Sheraton refers to the fact that, "wire doors are much introduced at present in cabinet work… they have generally green, white or pink silk fluted behind".

This suggests that the doors and the brass bits are very much a fashion thing of that period. But I can only think of pieces of furniture that we would now call chiffoniers, with the exception perhaps of side-cabinets, which have doors fitted with silk panels. Is it ridiculous to assume that the link to the name is merely the fabric in the door panels? Or is that just my simplistic, furniture restorer's mind at work?

What is certain though, is that many,

Edging repairs were effected using carefully chosen cross-grained veneers

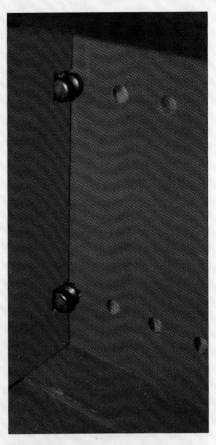

Pointer to quality: shelf support pegs are turned in solid rosewood

many chiffoniers, sideboards and cabinets were churned out in the Victorian period with essentially the same design as a Regency chiffonier, but these later pieces usually had arched panel doors.

Regency furniture is typically worth a great deal more than Victorian furniture, and Regency-style chiffoniers must have been in some demand, so the common latter-day 'improvement' was to remove the solid panels from the doors, square off the top of the frame and stick in some brass lattice-work and a swatch of silk to give them that Georgian look.

Brass gallery

If the 'chiffonier' started life as a sideboard or cabinet it would also need the addition of the shelf or shelves and a bit of brass gallery on top. Well a poor antique dealer has to earn a crust somehow doesn't he?!!

So back to the specimen in the workshop. It is not a Victorian improvement but an example of a quality Regency chiffonier and, by and

large, in pretty good condition. The feet are turned from solid rosewood with a bit of carving around the top. None had actually fallen off but they were all loose and needed re-gluing. Mind you, there was a little chunk missing from one, and this required a small repair.

It's interesting to see the effect of sunlight over the years. The outside faces of the feet – particularly the front ones – are that lovely golden colour that we associate with antique rosewood furniture. But the inner faces that have spent their lives tucked away under the cabinet, never seeing light of day, are almost black.

This blackness is not just hundreds of years of grime, but the true colour of freshly cut rosewood. When first made, this, and every other piece of rosewood furniture, would have looked a bit like ebony. Was it a source of great joy or great disappointment to the owner when a fine hand-crafted piece of purpley/black rosewood furniture slowly turned golden brown with lots of black lines? Perhaps the change was so gradual that nobody noticed.

Rosewood pegs

I was talking about doors earlier, and the doors on this piece are the classic silk and brass numbers with a nice split turned moulding forming the parting bead. Inside the cupboard is an adjustable shelf which in itself is hardly remarkable, but there is a nice touch which points to quality: the pegs which support the shelf are turned in solid rosewood.

Above the doors is a nicely executed moulding which is made up of two pieces. The top part would ave been encouraged into its basic ogee shape with a combination of planes and then carved. The lower section is a split turned moulding with a similar design to the parting bead; but notice how the two parts match perfectly.

The veneered edge above this moulding was a little damaged but repairs on a narrow edge with cross-grained veneers are pretty straightforward. It's really just a question of spending time choosing the right piece of veneer for the repair. ➤

Hand-cut, gilt-brass gallery demands careful cleaning

Ogee design would have been shaped by a variety of planes and then carved

Split turned moulding forms the parting bead

Hand cut

➤ The superstructure that forms the chiffonier's trademark shelf is prone to damage, as it is rather flimsy and doesn't respond well to the attentions of clumsy removal men. Moreover, the shelf assembly on this piece, whilst being in overall good condition, was flapping about all over the place and required me to dismantle it and re-glue.

The two columns that support the shelf are nicely turned and carved, once again in solid rosewood. However, the crowning glory is the pierced brass gallery. You would expect a gallery to be cast in sections, but on this piece the pattern has been cut by hand. If you look carefully at the outline and thickness of adjacent piercings they are slightly different and on close inspection, saw marks are visible on the inside faces.

You really wouldn't want to get out of bed in the morning if you knew that all the day had in store for you was more interminable gallery piercing!

You will see from the final photos that all the metalwork on this piece is nice and shiny, but the cleaning of brass or gilt gallery, mouldings or mounts, is another of those contentious issues which purists get seriously excited about – and with some justification.

Buffing

To clean or not to clean metalwork is a personal thing. Some people think bright fittings enhance a piece and some think this kind of skin-deep refurbishment looks completely wrong. On balance, dealers fall into the first camp. So as a restorer, if you work for dealers, like it or not, you are asked to

clean metal fittings.

But before you reach for the Brasso or rev up the buffing wheel, the important thing is to ascertain whether the items in question are covered in gold. If in doubt, the only intelligent – and safe – course of action is to assume that they are, and the critical thing from that point is to cut out any process that abrades, as any abrasion will very quickly remove gold and value along with it.

On this piece I removed the gallery, which was gilt, and spent many hours cleaning it with a liquid cleaner, a process which caused me to think that an "apprentice" might be a useful drudge to have in the workshop. Nevertheless, it did allow me to get in touch with the poor soul who had to cut the thing by hand a couple of hundred years ago! ∎

Fly leg in wind

ONE OF THE THINGS that keeps the likes of me in beer money, apart from the damage caused to furniture by people, children, dogs, cats, acts of God and removal men, is the fact that wood has the habit of continually moving. This was of course recognised hundreds of years ago.

Solution

The rather annoying thing, to me, is the fact that I am sure that we, in this country, noticed the effects of shrinkage on pieces of, albeit rather crude, furniture that were around in the 14th and 15th centuries – but the ground-breaking solution, which allowed the wood to move without trying to self-destruct, came from the continent. This was framed and panelled construction which seems to have come into this country in the second half of the 15th century, although it was not in general use until later in the 16th and early 17th centuries.

The benefits of framed and panelled construction, apart from counteracting shrinkage, were that pieces of furniture became much lighter, and consequently more portable, and used a great deal less wood.

The past

You don't come across a great deal of early oak furniture with movement problems because it was made from either quarter-sawn or riven timber. It will shrink but is unlikely to warp, and, as glue was not used a great deal, joints being held together with 'tree nails', the effect of glue deciding to let go was not a problem.

Later mahogany furniture however, is a different matter – wide boards were required which were cut from the full width of the tree, and so had the potential to warp. Add to this the fact that all of the timber used in those days was air dried and the furniture lived in draughty, cold houses. If you move this furniture into a modern centrally heated environment it may well decide to self-destruct!

"If you move this furniture into a modern centrally heated environment it may well decide to self-destruct!"

Modern times

Nowadays, of course, we have man-made boards that are used extensively as the main structural parts of much of the furniture that is produced. Shrinkage, when working with MDF, is hardly a consideration unless you are thinking of your own life expectancy and you enjoy inhaling the dust! But some makers still forget the basic principles and modern furniture also finds its way into restorers' workshops on occasion.

Challenge

So the challenge is how to deal with the bits that have gone out of shape in some way. This warping does not necessarily cause a structural problem – it may just cause an eyesore, and consequently make a piece of furniture less valuable.

A common problem that falls into the eyesore category is the fly leg on a fold-over card or tea table. The bit that warps is usually the moving arm with the leg on one end and a knuckle joint on the other. The arm is generally made from beech (*Fagus spp*), which is occasionally veneered on the outside face to make it look pretty. The effect of this piece going into wind is to throw the leg out of vertical and, because the leg is long, the twist in the arm, which may not be too severe on the face of it, is accentuated by the time you get to the foot.

Treatment

The leg/arm assembly has to be removed from the table to effect the flattening, and to do this the table top must be removed. This sounds simple, and sometimes is, but often the screws holding the top to the frame seem to weld themselves to the wood and more than a little persuasion and various cunning

ABOVE: Sawcuts relieve the tension for veneers to be inserted

RIGHT: Timber does move – this leg proves the point

"Shrinkage, when working with MDF, is hardly a consideration unless you are thinking of your own life expectancy and you enjoy inhaling the dust!"

> "The screws holding the top to the frame seem to weld themselves to the wood and more than a little persuasion and various cunning tricks are required to remove them"

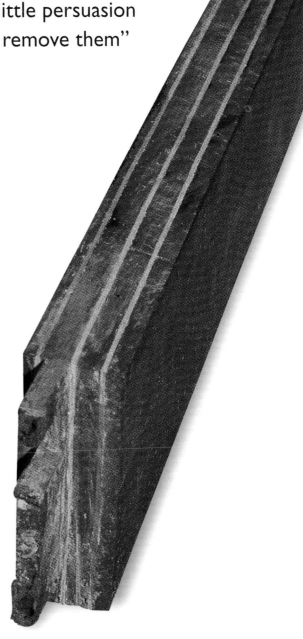

tricks are required to remove them. This achieved, the leg is removed. Use a parallel punch of a suitable size to drive the steel pin out of the knuckle joint. Make sure you support the underside of the joint whilst doing the driving unless you wish to learn the fine art of restoring broken knuckle joints – and watch out for the dreaded wood-worm which enjoys a bit of beech and seems to like living in knuckle joints, making them rather fragile!

Once the knuckle joint has been dismantled the leg is removed from the arm. The joint at this point is a mortice and tenon, which you hope is held together with very old, tired animal glue and can be persuaded to come apart with the introduction of a little heat and perhaps some water. Stick the arm into a vice with wood-lined jaws, and heave gently on the leg – note that false tenons are not covered in this article.

Flattening
Now, you could of course throw the arm away at this point, find a suitable piece of beech, and recreate the joints on the ends – which some people do. The problem with this approach is that, apart from the fact that it will take some time to re-make the joints, you are throwing away the original wood – and this, from a conservation point of view, is a heinous crime and should be avoided if at all possible.

The plan therefore is to flatten the existing arm. The system used in the flattening process is hardly ground breaking – if you want a piece of wood to take on a new shape, laminating is often the answer. This will not only persuade the arm to take on a new shape but it will also be very stable.

To achieve the laminating effect, several cuts have to be made in the existing wood which will then be filled with veneer of a suitable thickness. The cuts in the arm are made on the band-saw – on a thin arm, one cut either side of the tenon will be sufficient, but a thicker arm, such as on this table, will have room for three cuts.

The cut
The cut is made with the blade just skimming the cheek of the tenon and finishes about 20mm from the knuckle joint. In this way both the tenon and knuckle joints are preserved. The only slight problem with this system comes with the fact that you are, in all probability, using a long vertical fence to guide a twisted piece of wood! To overcome this, a new fence has to be hand crafted to hold the twisted arm vertical at the point adjacent to the blade, that is, at the point of the cut. This can be easily made from a piece of beech which is set vertically into a piece of MDF, with the vertical edge of the beech being fashioned into something of a point, against which the workpiece is held. The piece of MDF is made of sufficient size to enable it to be cramped easily to the table.

> "Watch out for the dreaded wood-worm which enjoys a bit of beech and seems to like living in knuckle joints, making them fragile!"

ABOVE: The result is a flat fly leg

LEFT: Nicely figured top to the table – which deserves a straight leg!

Sandwich

Having created the cuts in the arm, veneers of the same thickness as the cuts are required to fill the gaps, in the same wood as the arm is made from.

This done, mix up some Cascamite to stick the whole lot together. Cascamite is used because it does not allow any creep and, in my experience, is the most foolproof of adhesives for this type of work – it also has a nice long open time which makes for a more relaxed gluing experience.

The arm sandwich is now cramped to something which is flat and is not going to distort – a piece of old kitchen work-top or something similarly solid will fit the bill. It is worth checking at this point whether the various layers of the sandwich have stayed in register; if not, introduce a cramp at an appropriate place to persuade all the bits to get back into line.

Assembly

When the glue has set, remove the cramps, trim the veneers and assemble the leg, this time with animal glue. The rest of the assembly is a straightforward reverse of the dismantling process, and all that remains is to make the thin lines of veneer which are visible on the top and bottom faces disappear, using a suitable colouring system. In some cases, the top face is covered with baize to protect the top of the table when folded open, which will hide the repair. ■

Grins and grimaces

A restored card table ready for action again

WHEN YOU UNDERTAKE a piece of restoration work you need to bear in mind that what you are about to do to a poor innocent piece of furniture might affect its integrity, not to mention your own! The balance that we try to achieve between restoration and conservation is something that could be, and often is, discussed ad infinitum. If nothing else, it's a good excuse to talk shop whilst consuming large quantities of ale – public houses are the most conducive setting for this kind of discussion, you understand!

Grinning

Someone arrives at your workshop with a fold-over card table and says "It's grinning at me and I don't like it!" What they are referring to is a warp in the lifting part of the top – the grin being the gap between the two front edges which is caused by the front edge of the top leaf curling upwards. The bottom leaf is being restrained by the rest of the table and therefore tends to stay flat. The top leaf can also curl the other way which I suppose could be referred to

as a grimace. You have to learn an awful lot of technical terms in this game!

Decisions

Now some restorers will do the sucking air in through the teeth routine followed by any number of statements from "You can't do anything with that, Madam!", to "That looks expensive!". And a conservator would tell you to leave it alone or you'll be struck down by a thunderbolt!

On the assumption that the table's owner is feeling either rich or lucky or both, and the flattening of the offending bit of wood is to be undertaken, how can the flattening be achieved?

Flattening

One of the standard ways of flattening is to remove some of the

original wood, to take the tension out of the piece, and put some new wood back in. This can take the form of saw kerfing, which may work but is not always reliable – as can be seen in the photos.

You could, of course, remove all of the wood and replace it – removing the veneers and sticking them to new groundwork – but that is a little drastic and it is reasonable to assume that the bend could come back again at some point in the future. One of the reasons that the bend has occurred is that the table, being a card table, is veneered on one side only with the inside face being lined with baize – and you remember what your woodwork teacher told you about counter veneering. This might have been thought about by the table's maker who may have added cleats, but even cleats can't be relied upon to

"It is reasonable to assume that the bend could come back again at some point in the future"

RIGHT: A previous restorer had a go at kerfing, but it hadn't worked!

FAR RIGHT: Special router jig for flattening tops

stop all movement and even if they do, you will probably end up with a shrinkage problem!

What I do is to remove a chunk of the original wood and replace it with something stable, which is obviously more intrusive than kerfing but it does

have the benefit that it works, and you are still preserving all the original surfaces without

having to mess about with them in any way. The new bit will be covered with a baize liner.

"You remember what your woodwork teacher told you about counter veneering"

RIGHT: After routing, note step to prevent the joint telegraphing through the top veneer

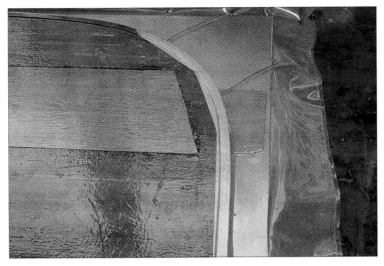

"The critical piece of equipment for this process is a router"

Router

The wood only need be removed from the part which is bent, which may mean the majority of the surface area or, as in this case, just a part of it. The critical piece of equipment for this process is a router which I use in conjunction with a jig made up of two rather large sections of angle iron and a few bits of wood. This jig is invaluable when the top to be flattened is badly warped as it will flatten it in the area being routed. It also minimises the risk of the router slipping – a router cutter coming out through an original veneered surface is embarrassing to say the least!

The router has the depth set to give a final cut that will remove at least ⅔ of the original groundwork, leaving a thickness of approximately 4 to 6 mm (⅛ to ¼in) of original groundwork/veneer depending on how brave you are feeling. It is just a question of progressing systematically across the area you have decided to remove, remembering to create a step at each end, to half the depth in the main area, to prevent the line of the join from telegraphing through to the top surface.

When the routing is finished the top will not be floppy – but it will be relatively easy to flatten it without too much pressure. Remember, if a lot of wood has been removed over a large area, the top will have become rather less robust than when it started and should be handled accordingly!

Replacing

So what are you going to stick back into the hole you have created? I like to use ply but MDF will certainly do the job – the important thing is that it is something stable.

When fitting the ply it is important that it is done with the top cramped down to a board to keep it flat which will ensure that the joints are nice and snug – if fitted when still warped, the joints will gape when cramped flat.

Use an off-cut of the ply to check the fit of the insert at the stepped section which, again, must be a snug fit to avoid any telegraphing through to the top surface. The adhesive I favour for gluing the insert into place is Cascamite because it allows a long open time and no creep – a vacuum bag is an excellent way of pressing the insert into place, although a large number of cramps will also do the job. Either way, something flat and fairly chunky is required to press or cramp onto.

Having waited the statutory six hours for the glue to cure, the top can be inspected for flatness. At this point any difference in level between the insert and the original surrounding groundwork will have to be resolved before reuniting it with the other half of the table.

Laying a new baize liner over the internal surface will complete the job, the surgery will be rendered invisible, and the value of the table should be enhanced! ■

LEFT: Glued-in and in the vacuum press

BELOW LEFT: A flat top!

BELOW: A useable card table again!

"A router cutter coming out through an original veneered surface is embarrassing to say the least!"

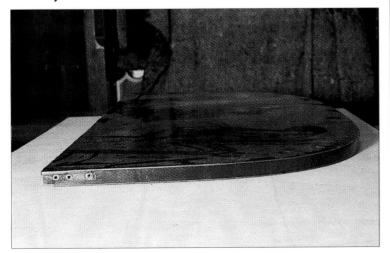

ABOVE: The strength of the warp in the panel has distorted the frame

ABOVE: Back of panel re-veneered with a balancing veneer to prevent re-occurrence of the problem

Another candidate for a bit of flattening was a corner cupboard that came into the workshop recently with some badly bent bits. The doors on the lower half of the cupboard, when shut, touched the carcass at the top but were in such severe wind that they were some 75 to 100mm (3 to 4 in) away at the bottom.

The door construction, on the face of it, seemed to be standard frame and panel, but in this case the panel was glued into the frame and had a moulding covering the joint on the front face – so if the panel wanted to move it

was going to take the frame with it!

To rectify this little problem, the doors had to be completely dismantled – which is easier said than done – and all of the component parts flattened. To flatten the stiles and rails, I used the same technique as was used on the card table fly-leg in the last chapter.

Panels

The panels, it would seem, were the cause of the twisting problem on these doors and had a huge amount of

tension in them. They were of quite a substantial thickness and, once again, had been veneered on only the front face, with no balancing veneer.

To flatten the panels required the removal of a large quantity of wood from the rear which was then replaced with something stable. The rear of the doors was veneered using Cascamite again, and all the bits were then put back together using Scotch glue.

The only additional process for the doors was the colouring required to blend the repairs to the original surfaces.

BELOW: There is no way that this will shut!

BELOW: A cupboard you can keep closed!

A stitch in time

The fretted 'dentil' detail that offended

"The implications of repairing a 20th century plywood rabbit hutch badly are not quite as onerous as doing the same to a 17th century oak food hutch!"

I'm sure it is something that I should have got used to by now, but there is hardly a week that goes by without my being amazed by the poor quality repairs that some people perform on very fine pieces of furniture. It's not just the lack of skill that surprises me but what can only be described as blind optimism – it is obviously felt that the mere act of doing something to a damaged item, however hideous the repair might look, will actually have the effect of improving it in some way. Improvement, after all, must be the initial motivation when repairing anything, be it a piece of antique furniture or something more modern – it's just that the implications of repairing a 20th century plywood rabbit hutch badly are not quite as onerous as doing the same to a 17th century oak food hutch!

Ownership

If the item in question is your own property then I suppose you might use the 'It's mine and I'll do what I like to it' argument – not that I would subscribe to this particular line of thinking, as it could be just a ploy to conceal Scrooge-like tendencies or a fear of furniture restorers. ➤

Fretsaw 'table' to take the work is made from MDF

Repair complete – coloured and polished

BELOW **Sawing out a new piece of moulding**

"If you're somewhere approaching six foot tall, the cornice is just about at eye level so it can be quite noticeable"

➤ To counter this argument, a conservator or restorer might suggest that you do not really 'own' an antique, even if you did have to hand over a large quantity of your hard-earned cash to become what you thought was an owner, you are in fact merely its guardian – and whilst it is in your possession it is your duty to care for it until it is passed on to its next guardian. Of course, as with most things, it is a question of applying a little common

sense as this argument is not necessarily relevant to all antiques – or is it?

Getting it right

There are of course plenty of people out there who buy antiques with the intention of enhancing their bank balances – they do a few repairs and then sell on, although some of these repairs are just so obvious that you have to wonder why they bothered. But then perhaps it is just that many people genuinely don't notice that one foot's the wrong shape or the grain in a veneer repair bears no resemblance to that surrounding it.

Seeing

To this day I still have the words 'Open your eyes!' ringing in my ears from the days when I was training – and the problem for most restorers, especially when newly qualified, is that

our eyes are so wide open that we notice the slightest little faults which can become a bit tiresome and potentially costly for the owner of a piece of furniture when he thought that he just needed a new handle and a rub of wax.

Meticulous approach

Sadly, I fear it's too late for me to change, and recently some repairs to a cornice moulding on a chest on chest jumped out and hit me right between the eyes. The offending part was the fretted 'dentil' part of the cornice – now this is hardly the most important part of this piece of furniture but, if you're somewhere approaching six foot tall, the cornice is just about at eye level so it can be quite noticeable.

The construction of this part of the moulding is very simple, it is just a piece of fretwork cut to form a regular profile

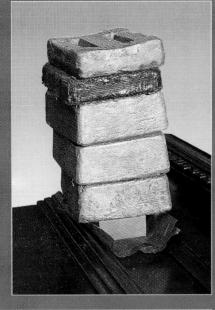

The striking colour difference between the drawers and the sides of the chest

with each 'tooth' having the same depth and width. A previous repairer of this piece obviously hadn't quite grasped this concept – at one point there seemed to be a tooth missing and at another a tooth had four sides instead of three. I found this far too annoying to leave and therefore set about sorting it out. I eased the offending bits off with a thin spatula and set about creating something that would fit a little better.

Repair

Having found a suitable piece of mahogany, I thicknessed it and cut it to width, marked out the profile of the teeth and then cut them out. This cutting out bit could be done with a power fret saw although it was not worth the effort of getting it out for this little bit, so I did it with my piercing saw.

To make this sort of job possible requires the use of a table to sit the work on – the table I used was an offcut of MDF with a wedge-shape taken out of one edge and a short batten fixed to the rear edge for holding the table in the vice. It was then just a question of holding the saw vertical and getting a rhythm going with the sawing hand whilst turning the workpiece to face the right direction with the other hand – it's a bit like rubbing your tummy whilst patting your head but it's a technique that's worth perfecting, especially if you don't own a power fret saw.

Shrinkage problem

Having successfully made a new section of moulding, it was just a question of doing a little whittling where the new and old bits met and then gluing into position. Before gluing the new bits on, I noticed that the section of cornice that formed the canted corner

"It's a bit like rubbing your tummy whilst patting your head but it's a technique that's worth perfecting, especially if you don't own a power fret saw"

was loose, and when viewed from above it was obvious that the cause was shrinkage. The corner was not difficult to remove and just required a little trimming before gluing back into position.

Cramping

Cramping is one of those things in life that easily gets unnecessarily ➤

"On this chest there was loose veneer below the cornice that required some glue and some pressure but it was not close enough to the edge to use a single sash cramp"

ABOVE **After colouring, a much healthier looking piece**

RIGHT **The finished chest**

➤ over-complicated – some people seem to delight in the challenge of seeing how many cramps they can introduce to any given cramping situation. Quite apart from the time and energy required to run round a workshop with armfuls of sash cramps, the chances are that a precarious arrangement for cramps will collapse and damage something or someone. So with this in mind, I always try to look for the simple solution to any cramping problem.

On this chest there was loose veneer below the cornice that required some glue and some pressure but it was not close enough to the edge to use a single sash cramp.

Thankfully, my brother in law, since marrying and having subsequently procured the obligatory two point four children has mysteriously curtailed his scuba diving activities. This left a weight belt that was looking for a new job and

lead weights are a very simple way of applying pressure to a hard-to-cramp surface! Silicone paper and a block of MDF were placed on the offending piece of veneer, and I then placed the lead weights on top, although a great pile that looks like the Eiffel Tower is probably a little unnecessary as it does have the potential of becoming more like the leaning tower of Pisa and collapsing, which would obviously not enhance the surrounding surfaces.

Colour

This chest on chest was a very good example of the bleaching effect that the sun can have on furniture. The drawer fronts were extremely pale when compared to the sides of the chests and looking at the drawer fronts it was interesting to see the 'shadow' from the swan neck handles where the handles had protected the wood from the sun.

Also, the areas behind the circular backplates were very dark and were pretty much the colour the whole piece would have been when it was first made – and there were dents in the drawer fronts caused by the bulbous part of the swan neck repeatedly hitting them over many years.

All of this was pretty conclusive evidence that the handles were original, but to make the whole piece look more balanced it was necessary to do something to the colour to blend the front of the piece to its sides. I cleaned the sides of the chests which had the effect of lightening them slightly, I then coloured the front faces to a final colour that was closer to the colour of the sides. Wax polish and a good deal of elbow grease resulted in a finished item that was hopefully conspicuous – but not because of the restoration work! ∎

Under the weather

If you were anything like my father, you'd take the owning of a barometer as an opportunity to add a little something to your nightly 'just before going to bed' routine. Write a note for the milkman; put the cat out; lock the doors; give the barometer glass a good rap with your knuckles to check what the weather has in store and off to bed!'

Having seen/heard this ritual barometer abuse going on for the many years I shared a roof with my father, I thought this was what barometers were all about. It's not terribly exciting but it gives walking down the hall a sense of purpose and there's a certain small

satisfaction in seeing the hand move a bit, even if the inscription the hand is pointing to seems to bear little relation to what the weather is doing or is about to do.

It was not until I became a furniture restorer that I was dissuaded from continuing with my barometer rapping activities. Hitting an antique barometer is not a good idea; it will do its weather predicting properties no good and may harm to its general well-being. When I took up the gentle art of offshore sailing I discovered the important thing about a barometer reading is not really what the hand is pointing at, but how quickly the hand is moving. If the

hand is moving at an alarming rate across the 'Set Fair' section it won't be set fair for very long!

A little history

Barometers came into being in the middle of the 17th century and were developed by a clever Italian chap called Torricelli; he was one of Galileo's boys so I suppose he can be forgiven for being clever. The first barometers were also known as 'baroscopes' or 'quicksilver weather-glasses' and were basically a column of mercury in a glass tube, the like of which you may vaguely remember from your physics lessons. Atmospheric pressure ➤

Close-up of the black 'blob' finial, the crowing glory to this mess

Reprofiled mahogany 'S' shapes glued on prior to recarving

➤ affected the height of the column and the height was read off a scale adjacent to the top of the column. To make the glass column of mercury a little more durable and aesthetically pleasing it was mounted on a long, narrow piece of timber and this long thinness looked something like a long-case clock, so it is no surprise that many of these early barometers looked very much like mini long-case clock cases!

Some of the more ornate examples of barometer cases were obviously designed to be hung on a wall where they would, like a long-case clock, be both decorative and functional. There were also barometers designed for the traveller who didn't want to get caught out in the middle of an unfriendly weather system; these are known as 'stick' or 'pillar' barometers which, as you might expect, are very slim to make them more portable and had less embellishments which might get damaged en route.

More history

There are various other types of barometer, but the one you are most likely to come across is the sort I'm working on this month, that is the 'wheel' or 'dial' barometer which, in this particular form, is also known as a 'banjo' barometer – no prizes for guessing why! These were popular towards the end of the 18th century and were often fitted with all sorts of additional knobs and functions to aid you in your quest for meteorological prowess. The built-in optional extras on this one are a hygrometer and a thermometer; there's also a spirit level to enable you to hang the barometer vertically and a convex mirror to enable you to check your wig is straight, some really flashy models were also fitted with a clock. These rather sophisticated barometers are rather like having The London Weather Centre hanging on your wall and they're probably just as accurate but have the benefit of being compact and looking rather lovely.

Handle with care

The fact these early barometers house glass tubes filled with mercury is something that must be considered when transporting them – and when restoring them. If someone were to snap-up one of these fine pieces of fore-casting equipment at their local auction house and casually lay it down in the back of their car to take home, the chances are in no time at all the car would be teeming with little silver balls, because one end of the glass tube is open! So, transport a barometer whilst it's being held vertically would appear to be the best idea, albeit not a very convenient one.

To make absolutely sure none of the silver stuff escapes it would seem sensible to seal the end of the glass tube with something. There's a tall, narrow door at the back of these barometers to enable access to the tube and if you're lucky you'll find a length of stiff wire with a small cork on the end lurking around somewhere; this will fit in the open end of the tube. To store a barometer in the workshop, hanging it on the wall is without doubt the safest place. When I come to do any work on one I always remove the mercury filled glass tube, having disconnected the dial mechanism and fitted the stopper. I'll then strap it to a suitable piece of plywood or MDF, which I then tuck away somewhere safe.

"The fact these early barometers house glass tubes filled with mercury is something that must be considered when transporting them – and when restoring them"

Carving completed, awaiting new patera

Careful work with a skew chisel. The reads are turned on the end of the bar of simulated ivory, forming the patera

The barometer

On this particular barometer the whole case was fairly sound, apart from the usual areas of loose veneer and stringing, but the area at the top around the broken pediment was looking a bit of a mess. This part of the case just didn't look right: the veneer just below the pediment was coarse grained, whereas the rest of the case had a very fine veneer, and the carving to the scrolls that made up the pediment just didn't work. One would expect the shape of the scrolls at the front forming the broken pediment would flow nicely into the side mouldings at their mitred joints, but concave bits on the front lined up with convex bits on the sides. The whole thing looked a bit of a dog's breakfast and the crowning glory to this mess was the black 'blob' finial!

The barometer's owner had noticed this area of the case didn't look quite right but wasn't quite sure why, so we got the books out and found some photos of similar barometers. The scrolls that made up the broken pediment were the wrong profile but in essence were the right overall shape; ➤

Patera

The small patera at the top ends of the scrolls would have originally been made from ivory, but because elephants are rarely seen in these parts and we are, of course, a highly politically correct workshop, I used simulated ivory. Simulated ivory comes in bar form and is convincing as far as colour and markings are concerned, unless you are studying it through your microscope. It can also be easily turned and carved. My experience with turning of this material is that quite a low speed is far less traumatic to both the turner and the bar. At high speed I find the 'ivory' bar has a tendency to grab at the chisels, removing rather bigger chunks than had been hoped for in the process. The profile to these patera is just a series of simple reeds, so having turned the bar down to the required finished diameter, I created the reeds on the end of the bar with a nice sharp skew chisel. A very steady hand is required for this, so consuming large quantities of shandy the night before is not to be recommended!

The finished patera

Patera glued in place

➤ this was borne out by the shape of the groundwork behind which was still original. The bits missing from this barometer – but fitted to all the similar barometers in my books – were the small turned ivory patera fitted to the ends of the scrolls; also the black 'blob' finial should have been a nice brass urn.

Handy work

To reprofile the scroll, I first removed the offending impostors and replaced them with some new bits of mahogany which I shaped roughly before gluing on. I then did the final carving and blending into the original side mouldings with them in situ. The important thing to keep at the forefront of your mind when carving an 'S' shape is that the grain direction at the surface is changing as you go round the curve – forget this at your peril! It's very obvious when your mind has drifted off to another place because a large irregular shaped chunk tears away from the surface instead of the fine curly shaving you were hoping for.

The other useful thing to have in your quest for success is a good selection of carving chisels. A chisel with exactly the right profile will give a nice crisp result.

If the wrong size chisel is used it will inevitably require sanding to achieve something close to the required shape!

Finish

The polish to the case had perished in places so I removed all the various fittings, repolished the case, blended in the new scrolls and veneer. At the owner's request I cleaned the brass fittings and, having fitted the new 'ivory' patera; I aged them a little by putting some 'dirt' into the valleys of the reeds.

Finally, I fitted the new urn finial and replaced all the workings.

It's probably still pretty unreliable for weather forecasting but hopefully it's a bit closer to its original appearance, despite having bits of plastic stuck to its pediment! ∎

With a new urn finial and good polish, the barometer was restored to something like its original glory

According to the rule

I HAVE ALWAYS rather liked the idea of designing an item of furniture and having it named after me. This is, of course, a rather pointless and self-indulgent thing to want, but Jupes managed it with his remarkable expanding table and, according to Sheraton, The Countess of Pembroke managed it with a table that also expanded, but rather less so, without the need for an ingenious mechanism.

Pembroke table
The Countess was apparently the first person to order a 'Pembroke' table in the middle of the 18th century. This sort of table was generally made with square tapering legs and was fitted with two fairly short flaps along the long edges which were supported on hinged wooden brackets, sometimes described as 'fly brackets'. The Pembroke is not to be confused with the Victorian 'Sutherland' which has a narrow top and long flaps along the long edge, supported on gate-legs.

Purpose
Sheraton described the Pembroke table as being suitable for a lady or gentleman to breakfast on, and I have to say that eating your Weetabix from a piece of polished satinwood must be a much more uplifting way to start the day than from a piece of Formica.

A development of the Pembroke was the Harlequin Pembroke which had a sort of box fitted with drawers that was hidden within the body of the table. This structure was raised using weights or springs and could transform your breakfast table into a writing or drawing table which was apparently a very suitable accoutrement for a lady's boudoir.

"Eating your Weetabix from a piece of polished satinwood must be a much more uplifting way to start the day than from a piece of Formica"

"Rule joints were originally cut using a matched pair of planes, one to form the concave part, the other the convex"

ABOVE: The top removed – note damaged corner

ABOVE RIGHT: The area above the hinge had broken out, causing damage on both sides

BELOW: In order to keep the repair strong, a dovetail splice is used – cut with a fine saw

"Pembrokes were made in large numbers in the last decade of the 18th century and, about this time, a variation evolved from it in the form of the sofa table"

Sofa table

Pembrokes were made in large numbers in the last decade of the 18th century and, at about this time, a variation evolved from it in the form of the sofa table. The sofa table was longer and, again, had short flaps to extend it, but this time they were fitted to the short sides which were also supported on hinged wooden brackets.

The sofa table was designed to be placed, not surprisingly, in front of a sofa and was used by ladies to draw, read or write on. Nowadays sofa tables often seem to find themselves positioned behind sofas where they are used as a means of displaying little silver treasures and wedding photographs.

Hinges

The hinges used with a rule joint are 'table hinges', sometimes referred to as 'back-flap table hinges', the distinctive feature being that the two flaps of the hinge are of unequal length and the countersinking of the screw holes is on the opposite side to the knuckle. The hinge is fitted with the knuckle buried in the underside of the table top with the pin centre placed at the centre of the quadrant which forms the rule joint.

This means that there is not very much wood left above the knuckle and so that area of the hinge is rather fragile and will occasionally disintegrate. The result is that the nice clean line of the rule joint is somewhat marred by an area of splintered wood with the hinge peeking out.

The fragile part of the concave side of the joint on the flap is along the top edge where the wood is at its thinnest, and if this bit is going to get damaged it is usually at the end. To effect a repair to this is just a question of splicing a piece on and shaping as necessary. The repair to the convex part over the knuckle of the hinge is a little more involved.

Modern technology – the router will cut a flat bottom but a less noisy cut can be done by hand

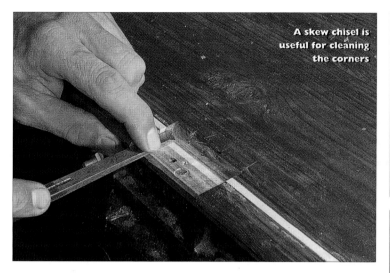

A skew chisel is useful for cleaning the corners

Dismantling

The table I am working on here is a Pembroke in rosewood with a wide satinwood banding. It has a small area of damage to the end of the rule joint on the leaf, and an area above one of the hinges has broken out.

The first thing that must be done is to remove the top from the frame which usually involves removing about half a dozen screws. I always mark the frame and the top with masking tape so that I know which way round it is meant to go when it comes to putting it all back together again. I also label the screws and hinges and their respective homes. This is necessary for the screws

because when they were hand-made they were all slightly different, and with the hinge screws in particular, it is usual to find a large variation in their size. The labelling of screws at this stage will mean that there is much less weeping and wailing later – which is, of course, undignified behaviour, even in a workshop.

TOP: Rosewood and pine laminated block for the splice

ABOVE: The block in place

"The labelling of screws at this stage will mean that there is much less weeping and wailing later – which is, of course, undignified behaviour, even in a workshop"

RULE JOINT

A feature that the Pembroke, the sofa, and the Sutherland table have in common is that there is usually a rule joint along the edge where the flaps meet the top. Not that rule joints weren't used before this – they had been in use since about 1660 on drop-leaf tables and were a much neater way of joining a leaf to a top than the earlier square edges that formed a rather clumsy-looking right angle at the table's edge when the flap was down.

Rule joints were originally cut using a matched pair of planes, one to form the concave part, the other the convex. The modern equivalent is, of course, a pair of matched router cutters – same effect, more noise, less skill!

RIGHT: The anatomy of the rule joint

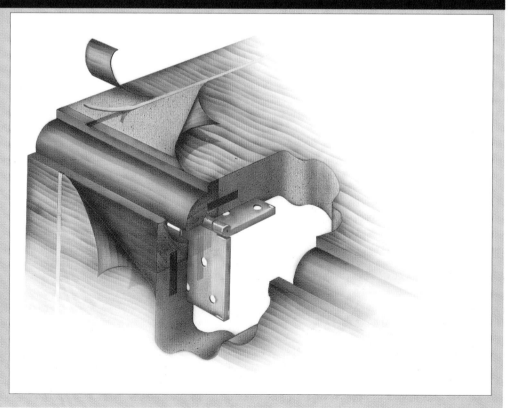

Surgery

ABOVE: A carving chisel is used to form the housing for the knuckle of the hinge

ABOVE RIGHT: A bowed flap caused the re-fitted hinge to bind

BELOW LEFT: The solution – slot out the countersinks, allowing the hinge to move

BELOW RIGHT: The completed repair from the user's side with enough clearance to avoid the two halves rubbing

The surgery to the rule joint is performed from the underside of the table and a dovetail insert is required at the area of the damage. The underside of the top is marked with lines running back at right angles from the edge, just beyond the extremity of the damage, and cuts are then made along the lines with a fine saw. These cuts are made at an angle to create the dovetail housing and the housing should extend back at least as far as the first line of hinge screw holes.

At this point there is an opportunity to apply a little modern technology in the form of a router to remove the waste and create a nice flat bottom to the housing. But, in the time it takes you to find the router and spanners and fit an appropriate bit, you will have been able to perform the same operation several times with a nice wide chisel – your ears won't hurt, you won't have dust up your nose, and you would have that warm inner glow of a craftsman – the choice is yours!

Even if a router is used, some hand work is still required to clean out the housing at its edges – a skew chisel can be useful to get into the back corners. Don't be tempted to use a dovetail router cutter to create the housing all in one go – you will end up with the rule joint breaking out at the edge and it will inevitably end in tears.

Insert

Having created a housing, something is required to stick in it – on this table I laminated a piece of rosewood to some pine, as this was the way the table was constructed. I made the insert a little oversize in all dimensions and then offered it up to the edge of the housing and scribed the angled lines of the housing – these lines were then extended back at right angles.

When I had transformed the insert into a dovetail shape I offered it up to the housing. At this stage it was still too thick to actually fit but, because it was oversize, I had the opportunity to make adjustments without having to start again.

Shaping

Having achieved a perfect fit, the insert was glued into place and when the glue had set it was time for a little shaping. The first stage was to trim the surface of the insert flush with the underside of the table, I then extended the lines of the rebate for the hinge flap to the edge and, having re-created the rebate, I offered the hinge up and marked the position of the knuckle.

A carving chisel was required to form the housing for the knuckle of the hinge and the shaping of the radius of the quadrant was done last with a combination of cranked chisel and shoulder plane.

Fitting

At this stage I re-fitted the flap to see if everything worked – and it didn't. The damaged area of rule joint had been over the middle of the three hinges and it became apparent that the reason for the damage was that the flap was bowed. The top was also bowed which meant that the flap had an acceptable fit when it was raised but the mid point of flap wanted to move away from the edge of the table when it was lowered.

To overcome this problem I decided that the only thing to do was to slot the screw holes in the hinge on the flap side. I didn't do the screws up too tightly and this resulted in the hinge being able to move as necessary when the flap was raised and lowered without it going into self-destruct mode again.

I checked that there was clearance between the two halves of the rule joint at the site of the repair as it is more than a little annoying to find that your colouring and polishing, that blends the repair, disappears because the two halves are rubbing.

A partridge in a pier table

Sorely in need of treatment, the table had long been neglected

Strong and robust, the ornately carved legs remained intact

When discussing a piece of furniture with a potential client it is very important, as a restorer, that you enhance your credibility at every available opportunity, and one area of possible enhancement is wood identification. Most people are pretty good at spotting mahogany, walnut and oak but when a restorer or an auction-house catalogue describes a piece of furniture as being made from 'fruit wood' you know they're struggling a bit, as this term is hardly specific.

Honesty

Not that this sort of behaviour is entirely surprising – this was brought home to me several years ago when I shared a workshop with a restorer who had many more years of experience than I. One day I called him over to look at a table with an unusual veneer on its top. The table had been in my possession for a few days and I just couldn't decide on what wood it was made from. When faced with the table, he looked at it for a few minutes, talked about how nice the legs were and what a good specimen it was of its type – classic stalling behaviour – then, to my dismay, he scratched his head and said, "Do you know how many hundreds of different species of wood there are in the world?" and with that he walked off.

This was not taken as being particularly helpful at the time but upon reflection actually gave me some degree of comfort, although this is not the sort of reply that should be given to an inquisitive potential client unless, of course, you don't want his custom!

Wisdom

Another way of dealing with the thorny question of wood identification is covered by the adage, 'If in doubt,

The moulding is completed by using a shoulder plane

Mouldings

There was a length of moulding missing from around the top edge of the base which I had to replace. At the mention of missing mouldings, restorers immediately reach for a steel offcut, some files and a scratch stock and spend an hour or so creating a cutter. Whilst this is often the appropriate thing to do, it is not always necessary. This moulding was quite simple in that it consisted of one step and a convex curve. I cut a length of rosewood a little oversize and started the shaping by cutting the step on the router table. This done, I put it in a vice and introduced the curve with the help of a No 92 shoulder plane.

Of course it helps to have something to guide you whilst shaping, so I took a mould from the existing moulding with a piece of Plasticine and transferred the shape to the ends of my piece of rosewood. The secret to shaping using this method is to use a plane with a sharp blade, and to take even cuts along the whole length of the moulding each time — if you pick at it, it will end up a wiggly mess, and rosewood isn't cheap!

Having achieved a shape that was close to the original, I cut the mitre and glued it in place doing the final shaping in situ to exactly match the existing moulding where they met at the mitre.

➤ be specific – if you can also sound supremely confident.' There is a story, which may even be true, which is set in a restorer's workshop – the boss is discussing a piece of fine furniture with a dealer and the wood used for the bandings is being debated at some length. At this point an old chap with silver hair and sporting a tatty old apron and half-rim spectacles, who has been restoring for the company since time began, happens to pass. On hearing the discussion he takes one look at the bandings, says "That's partridge wood, that is!" with great conviction and walks off with a 'don't young people today know anything?' look on his face. The pair are left in stunned silence, so impressed are they at this display of knowledge, and satisfied that this query has been resolved beyond any possible doubt, they move on to other matters. Later, when the dealer has left, safe in

the knowledge that even if the owner of the company knew nothing about wood, at least he had had the sense to surround himself with highly-trained artisans who did, the boss went to his trusty old restorer and congratulated him on his boundless knowledge. The old man peered over his half-rim specs and said, "I always say it's partridge wood when I don't have a clue what it is!"

This seems to prove that a restoration workshop, if it's going to get anywhere, should have at least one restorer among its number who wears half-rim specs and is good at playing poker – I know mine has!

Accurate naming

Another requirement of a restorer is that he is able, when presented with a piece of furniture, to accurately give it a name. If you call a 'dumb waiter' a 'whatnot' and your client has just found

a similar piece in his Miller's described as a dumb waiter, he may begin to question your credibility. Which leads me on to 'pier tables' and 'console tables' – I was recently asked by a client to pick up a 'buffet' which I referred to as a 'console table', while a restorer in my workshop described it as a 'pier table'. This is the piece we are working on this month. The client was sadly mis-informed – but the question remains, is it a console or a pier table?

Console or pier

The console table seems to have originated from Italy and was an ornamental side table with an ornate base, often gilt, and fitted with a marble top. In this country they were made in the 18th and 19th century and were used to furnish formal reception rooms.

One of my books describes a console as being a piece of furniture with no

The table was used as a paint store for a number of years!

"The old man peered over his half-rim specs and said "I always say it's partridge wood when I don't have a clue what it is!"

Spirit paint stripper revealed the figure below

back legs which was screwed to the wall. The pier table was made in this country in the same period – and was nothing to do with large wrought iron structures that stick out into the sea in Brighton – they were a rich man's side table, designed to stand in front of a 'pier', which is the bit of wall between two windows. They were usually made in pairs and Mr Sheraton describes them as being "merely for ornament under a glass" – the glass being a 'pier glass' which was a mirror hung on a pier to reflect as much light as possible into the room. All of which seems very

straightforward until you look in another book – by the same author — which has pictures of console tables with back legs!

So in my opinion a console table is an ornate side table with or without back legs with a marble top, and a pier table is an ornate sided table, usually half-round, made in pairs and designed to sit under a pier glass!

Alternative uses

The table I am working on here is in the sort of condition that I relish. It is in rosewood and has the most wonderful

carved front legs but is looking very much the worse for wear and has obviously been used to store tins of paint for some considerable time.

As is often the fate of large pieces of furniture, it was designed for a large, grand room in a large, grand house but was too big to move to a smaller home, and therefore was left in an outbuilding where it got used in a less than appropriate way. Perhaps this table's previous owner was a fellow of some style who found that only vast chunks of carved rosewood could induce him to partake in the delights of DIY. Just ➤

Once polished, the glorious colour and figure come into their own

"I was recently asked by a client to pick up a 'buffet' which I referred to as a 'console table', while a restorer in my workshop described it as a 'pier table'"

The finished table is a big improvement

➤ imagine how much more inspired you would be to undertake a decorating job if your paint were stored in such an uplifting environment!

Repair work

Apart from the obvious poor state of the polished surfaces and the lack of a piece of marble, the table is made of such gargantuan proportions that it was still very sound. The base was a little the worse for wear as it had obviously been standing on a damp floor for some time. The softwood ground was now dry, but was a little soft, and to deal with this I applied some hardener which had the desired effect. Much of the veneer to the base was either loose or missing but the groundwork was now in a fit state to be glued to and I removed all the loose veneer, which was quite thick saw-cut, and re-glued it with Scotch. I patched it as necessary with some rosewood cut to

the appropriate thickness on the bandsaw from the solid. The actual structure of the base had suffered from the damp and I had to remove the glue blocks that remained and re-glue them, replacing any missing ones with new ones of a similar design.

Finishing

The only other small consideration was to make the table look pretty again. This was not an appropriate moment to reach for the belt sander – it rarely is! – because the abrasion would quickly turn the rosewood black – or mahogany red or walnut browny purple.

The chances are that under all the paint and grime there will be some lovely faded surfaces, but to get to them requires something that is gentle, and the only thing that really fits the bill is paint stripper, which is not only effective but requires little effort!

I applied the spirit-washable type of stripper to avoid any problem with the grain raising – and out from under the grime appeared wonderful oxidised rosewood! There were a few small problem areas that were a little light, but nothing that couldn't be resolved with a paintbrush and a little colour.

Having neutralised the stripper I polished the table with shellac followed by wax to complete the transformation from paint pot stand to elegant rosewood console table – or should I say partridge wood pier table? ■

A century since

GONE ARE THE DAYS when a furniture restorer would take himself off to his local auction house and buy a van load of Victorian furniture with the intention of taking it back to the workshop and turning it into 'breakers' – this being the gentle art of breaking pieces of furniture up for use in the restoration of other pieces more worthy of being restored.

In those days, which are in fact not that long ago, Victorian furniture was rather looked down upon and was consequently very competitively priced – it was,

however, often made from remarkably good timber and veneer, with nicely faded and patinated surfaces, and could be used successfully for patching up, often retaining these original surfaces.

Modern outlook
Time moves on, and early Victorian furniture is now over 160 years old. A lot of it is very well made, and its value has increased. If a restorer buys Victorian furniture now, he usually takes it back to his workshop for restoration and selling on – it would be a wealthy

restorer who could afford to break Victorian furniture these days and sadly, or perhaps fortunately, the words 'wealthy' and 'restorer' are not commonly uttered in the same breath!

Then there is, of course, the question of ethics relating to the dismantling of our heritage. Restorers that are being trained today would not be able to sleep at night if they developed murderous tendencies towards furniture which, through no fault of its own, was created in the wrong part of the wrong century.

"The words 'wealthy' and 'restorer' are not commonly uttered in the same breath!"

Eclectic

Having said all that, not all Victorian furniture is wonderful by any stretch of the imagination. The population was growing, and a great deal of furniture was required by the new middle class. Machines sped up production, but what was produced was, sometimes, what might be referred to by some as eclectic – others might describe it as a rather bizarre mess, being a combination of many earlier styles, all included in one piece of furniture.

This was presumably acceptable, because the new middle class did not have a particularly educated taste in the furniture department, perhaps because they did not have the benefit of swanning around the continent for months on end, taking in classical design. Consequently, some furniture looked extremely odd – with some being replicas of previous styles, and all varying enormously in quality.

Stylistically, this period can be confusing for a potential collector, but what is clear is that Victorian, and indeed Edwardian, furniture is now extremely popular – and in terms of increased value, according to the Antique Collectors' Club, it seems to be out-performing antique furniture as a whole.

Writing table

Not surprisingly, the piece of furniture that I have been working on this month comes from this period. It is a writing table which is made from oak, with burr oak veneer to the top and the frieze.

Apart from the overall design of a piece, it is useful when trying to date furniture to know when particular design features were introduced. On this piece, one pointer is the quadrant drawer slips which were introduced around 1820 – which of course doesn't make it Victorian (1837-1901) but it tells us that it is post-1820, and other elements of the piece can tell us how post 1820 it is.

Muntin detail

This is a well put together piece and, still looking at the drawer which is made from quarter sawn oak, it has a nice detail at the muntin, which has its top surface flush with the drawer bottoms with a single reed running down each edge.

At some time in its life, this drawer experienced someone who was having a seriously bad day with their fountain pen.

"At some time in its life this drawer experienced someone who was having a seriously bad day with their fountain pen"

Something missing

At each end of the frieze drawer, on the actual frieze, was a section with three vertical flutes carved into it, and just below the flutes was a distinct line and the remains of some glue – so there was obviously something missing.

This missing section lined up with the ebonised mouldings that ran along the bottom of the frieze, and the frieze drawer. But the glue line showed that the missing bit was wider than the ebonised bits, and this section of the frieze was standing slightly forward of the frieze and drawer, either side of it.

So, the dilemma was, what did the missing bits look like? They could not have been a straight continuation of the moulding because they were

definitely wider, and the ground for these bits was not flush. My first thought was that they would also be ebonised, and would have a rectangular section, with the grain running along their length – the width being dictated by the glue line, and the thickness being such that the mouldings were all flush.

I duly made them up, ebonised and fitted them – and they were obviously wrong. It was time to take the dog for a walk with the hope that a little canine-induced inspiration would be forthcoming. An hour of tramping around the Sussex countryside with my spotty lunatic had the desired effect and, on my return, I made up two new pieces of moulding of the same shape, but this time in oak, with the

grain running vertically, and no ebonising. All of which goes to prove that workshop dogs are vital, and their running costs should be tax deductible!

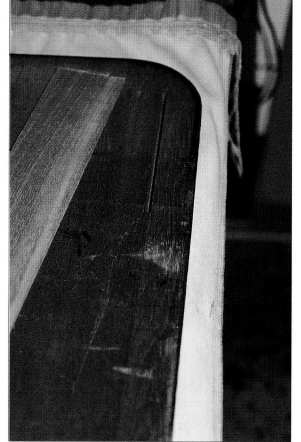

High tech – steam machine for loosening the split mouldings

Shrinkage

Other areas that required attention were caused by that old favourite, shrinkage. The construction of the top consisted of a piece of mahogany, with oak glued to its edges, forming the moulding. As usual, the long grain moulding ended up having a fight with the shrinking mahogany it was fixed to and, as is always the case, the oak moulding won, and splits appeared.

I decided that the least intrusive way to deal with this was to get the router out and, using a cutter that just spanned the split at its widest point, run it along the line of the split and drop a piece of mahogany into the resulting groove.

Moulding

Below the top, and running along the top edge of the frieze, was another moulding, this time ebonised. The designer/maker of this table gave himself a golden opportunity to avoid shrinkage problems but obviously was not a man to take an easy option when it presented itself. This moulding was made up as a separate frame which was screwed to the top of the frieze – the frame consisting of oak pieces jointed at the corners, and the pieces forming the moulding were then fixed to it with a loose tongue.

The pieces running along the long sides of the frame were fine, as the grain in both pieces ran in the same direction but, as a result of a rather misguided flash of Victorian inspiration, the moulding along the short sides was fitted as a cross-grain moulding, and was now enhanced by many splits of varying thickness.

Because the moulding was only fixed along one edge and was several inches wide, the splits were not parallel, and therefore it was not possible to just take it all apart, shunt all the bits together and re-glue it.

Remedy

The first step was to take all the cross-grain moulding off the frame – to achieve this I used one of our high

ROUTER JIG

As there were many pieces to deal with, it was worth spending a little time making up a jig for the router. The idea was to hold each pair of adjacent pieces in a way that a router cutter could be run between them, creating parallel gluing faces. To ensure that the pieces would be in register when glued back together, a piece of wood was machined up, with a groove in it, to match the tongue on the back of the moulding. The two adjacent pieces of moulding were then mounted on the groove, with the distance between them being just less than the width of the router cutter.

Everything was held in position with an arrangement of G-clamps and sash cramps and a fence for the router was fixed on top. This had to be a systematic process as keeping all the bits in order is very important if everything is to finally line up correctly.

The effect of shrinkage, and the removal of a certain amount of wood with the router, resulted in an embarrassing gap at the end of the two lengths of moulding, which was filled with two new pieces of wood, hand-crafted to blend.

ABOVE: Router jig for re-aligning the mouldings – note the grooved board for holding in place

tech pieces of equipment to produce some steam. It consists of an electric hot-plate, an old 5 litre tin can containing some water, a length of plastic hose, a fairly large bore syringe needle with the point ground off, various bits for jointing it all together, and a cork to prevent any of your tender bits getting burnt.

Lots of steam in the area of the joint, and a considerable amount of patience, ultimately had the required effect. It was then just a question of trimming all the sides of the splits so that they would go back together again.

Ebonising

Ebonising is a technique often used by restorers, who are less than gifted in

the finishing department, to blend their repairs. It can therefore be assumed that it is a pretty straightforward technique and it just involves using anything that will make the desired piece black. This could involve the use of chemicals, black paint, black pigment in some sort of vehicle, black spirit stain in your polish, or a combination of all four. I, on this occasion, used a combination of paint and black polish.

A lot of the ebonised bits needed touching up in this way. The rest of the table, which was covered with thick gloopey coloured polish, which was damaged and obscuring the grain, was re-polished to make it a vision of Victorian loveliness. ∎

All the cards on the table

SOME TIME AGO a client came into the workshop with a rather nice Regency rosewood fold-over card table which he had bought at auction. The top was split right down the middle – and was held precariously together by the veneer on one side and a piece of baize on the other. Even though the veneer was saw-cut, and consequently quite thick, it looked like it had just about had enough of this additional task – after all it's a bit much when your original job spec was just to look pretty!

Negotiation

The two boards that made up the top were cupped, which gave the table an odd 'grimacing' look when closed. I pointed this out to the client and explained, if a little vaguely, that this could be rectified by flattening – at which point, he demanded to know how I could possibly justify performing such intrusive surgery on a fine piece of antique furniture. To make matters worse, I then suggested that the table needed re-polishing – this was read as meaning that I would be taking his fine antique to the local stripper for a dip in the caustic tank followed by a couple of coats of Polyurethane!

ABOVE LEFT:
Honeysuckle
design in the
centre of the
frieze with some
of the damaged
inlay

ABOVE RIGHT:
Damaged brass
inlay around the
Coromandel
crossbanding on
the top

"At which point, he demanded to know how I could possibly justify performing such intrusive surgery on a fine piece of antique furniture"

At this stage of the negotiation, I began to wonder where it would end – but the outcome was that the client persevered and I ended up with the limited job of fixing the top, letting in a few patches, re-laying some of the loose veneer, and giving it a new piece of baize.

Function

When the client came to collect the table a few weeks later, he initially seemed quite pleased but became rather preoccupied with the fact that, with the top now glued together, the grimace was more pronounced. When split, the top had, in effect, collapsed in the middle onto the lower leaf which meant that the two halves of the curve looked less severe. When the table was in its closed position it looked quite acceptable but, having opened the top to reveal the baize, one edge was found to be sticking up in

the air and I gave the advice that if any weight were put on the open leaf it would strain the hinges. It was at this point that the client told me that he wanted to use the card table for playing cards on – something that had not occurred to me that people still actually did! Naturally, when fully restoring a piece of furniture, I return it to its original condition – and the use it was designed for. It taught me to ask a few more questions!

Another table

Quite recently a client brought a similar Regency rosewood card table into the workshop, again in need of some care and attention – it had Coromandel crossbanding and some rather nice brass inlay including a honeysuckle design in the centre of the frieze. As is often the way when you stick metal into wood across the grain, the brass had buckled – this can happen even if there is no shrinkage in the wood – brass just sometimes feels the need to escape.

Buckled brass

To deal with the buckled brass stringing in the top surface required that the brass be removed so that it could be straightened and shortened. Straightening brass stringing is not as easy as you might think – but after many years in the business, and many high-tech failures, I have perfected the process.

The ingredients for success are two pieces of wood and a hammer – sandwich the stringing between the pieces of wood and annoy the chap working on the bench next to you with seemingly incessant hammering. These pieces of stringing had a curve at one end, so the obvious place to attempt the shortening was at the other end, which was straight, with a mitre cut at its end. The new mitre was cut with a junior hacksaw, bearing in mind that too long is easier to rectify than too short, and any adjustments can be carried out with a file.

RIGHT: The
invisible repair

FAR RIGHT: New
brass blank, fixed
with double-sided
tape to MDF to
achieve a clean
cut on the
bandsaw

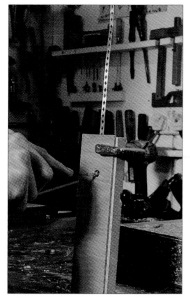

Scarfe joint

A curved section of the stringing had
been subject to some previous repair
work which was looking very much
the worse for wear and had been
secured, unsuccessfully, with brass
pins rather than glue. I decided to
sacrifice the damaged section, which
was the curved part at the end, but, as
with box or any other stringing, a butt
joint was rather too obvious – the
only appropriate joint was a scarfe.

Before thinking about joints,
though, it was important to adjust the
replacement stringing to exactly the
right width, with a little filing. The
next stage was to create the curve,
which was done over a shaped
former, then the mitre and scarfe were
hacksawn and filed to a perfect fit!

Brass inlay

The brass inlay on the frieze was
pierced, and quite a large section of it
was either damaged or missing. The

"The client told me that he wanted to
use the card table for playing cards on –
something that had not occurred to me
that people still actually did!"

original piercing was constant in both
size and spacing which pointed to it
having been punched out, but I had
to resort to replicating it by hand.

Firstly, I cut lengths of the correct
thickness brass to width on the band
saw with a ½in 24 tpi blade – this is,
in fact, a blade for cutting wood but
it has no trouble at all getting
through soft metals. To get a nice
crisp cut on the bandsaw, I mounted
the brass on a piece of MDF with
some double-sided sticky tape and

made minor adjustments with a file.

The next stage was to accurately
mark the positions of the piercing
and then drill a hole of the
appropriate size at each position. I
looked at various ways of
completing the shaping and decided
that a warding file would be
effective. To hold the brass steady
and vertical whilst in the vice I made
a piece of MDF with a groove run in
it, put a piece of ply on top to form a
sandwich, and made a hole through

"Sandwich the stringing between the
pieces of wood and annoy the chap
working on the bench next to you with
seemingly incessant hammering"

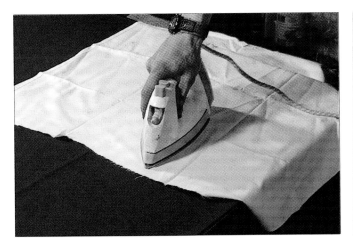

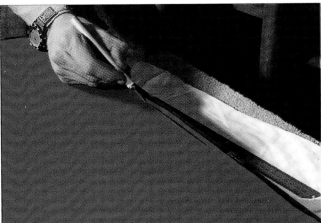

both, through which to file. This operation is one of those mind-numbing ones so not too many piercings were done in one go! Old wives and old woodworkers 'etch' brass by rubbing it with a piece of garlic before gluing it in place with Scotch glue – this rather eccentric behaviour certainly won't do any harm, but my learned friend in the workshop, who has a degree in furniture restoration, assures me that it won't do any good either, and he should know!

Tops

The tops of the table had split and one leaf had been repaired with butterflies – I have never been convinced by this method of stabilising a split and this scepticism was borne out by the fact that the split had opened up again.

Removing the butterflies, however, seemed a little pointless so I just routed along the length of the split between the butterflies, as deep as I dared without coming through the veneer on the other side, and glued in some suitable pieces of mahogany with Scotch glue.

Final operation

The final operation, apart from the finishing, was to lay a new piece of baize, if for no other reason than to cover up the repairs – in my experience, the only way to get good quality baize is to buy it from a firm that makes or repairs snooker tables.

Having found the right baize, it needed to be glued, and the traditional glue for this is Scotch – although you could use PVA or even wallpaper paste. I removed all the remnants of the old covering and its adhesive, and sized the surface with a weak solution of Scotch glue. When this was dry, I cut the baize to approximately the right size and covered the surface with Scotch glue of the sort of consistency you would use for veneering. Next, I placed the

"The next stage was to create the curve, which was done over a shaped former, then the mitre and scarfe were hacksawn and filed to a perfect fit"

baize on top and smoothed it out with my hands. I heated up the iron and, using a piece of old sheet between the iron and the baize, went over the whole surface paying particular attention to the edges.

The next bit required a steady hand and a very sharp scalpel, bearing in mind all the time that knife marks across the surrounding veneer would not be appreciated, and neither would gaps between the baize and the veneer. Problems occur if the baize is not properly stuck at the edge as it will move with the blade – it will look great while you are cutting but will spring away from the veneer when you have finished the cut.

Having finished the trimming, I folded the table to the closed position but held it open slightly with an offcut to allow any moisture out. I left it in this position overnight – and in the morning it was ready for the cards! ■

"The original piercing was constant in both size and spacing which pointed to it having been punched out, but I had to resort to replicating it by hand"

After the bodgers

I DON'T THINK there are many people who would want antique chairs dotted around their house with V&A style 'Don't sit on me or I'll collapse!' tapes running from the cresting rail to the seat rail – but equally, there are many of us who are guilty of chair abuse which results in the need for some sort of maintenance, unless the chair is of a very sturdy construction.

Time for action

Abuse of any chair, particularly the rather more fragile forms of the 18th and 19th century, will of course put strain on the joints which, over time, will become loose. This is more quickly evident in chairs with drop-in seats as there is no upholstery to hold the seat frame together. A stuff-over seat may get a little support from the upholstery but it does have the disadvantage that the seat rails are generally made from beech. If the dreaded worm has eaten its way through your tenons, your chair is guaranteed to be in trouble.

"There is only one real option open for a damaged chair, and that is to take the chair apart, clean the joints, and put it together again with foul-smelling hot sticky stuff"

The bodgers

There is only one real option open for a damaged chair, and that is to take the chair apart, clean the joints, and put it together again with foul-smelling hot sticky stuff. The route that many people take is to introduce some metal into the joints which can take the form of a screw, or several screws if someone large is coming to lunch, a metal bracket at any junction that looks vaguely right-angular, a nail or two if you don't possess the required technology for screws – or if you're a bodger with conservational tendencies, some wooden dowels may enable you to sleep at night!

ABOVE: Chairs are long suffering pieces of furniture!

ABOVE: Hessian can hide some unpleasant surprises

"Something else that is often found under upholstery is glue-soaked hessian wrapped around the front seat rail joints – and be warned, you will rarely find a pleasant surprise under hessian-encased joints!"

ABOVE: A single screw is a fairly minor problem compared to some you might find!

BELOW: Hidden horrors beneath the hessian

The screws and dowels are attempting to stitch the mortice and tenon joints together, and this may of course have the desired effect for a time, but the day will surely come when the job will have to be done properly. The trouble is that all the drilling, screwing, and doweling will have made a mess of the mortices and tenons and when the joint becomes mobile again, the lumps of metal that have been introduced are likely to make the tops of the legs split around the mortices.

Brass tacks

If a chair is to be taken apart, upholstery will have to be removed – and upholstery can hide many horrors. The next step is to check for that metalwork – brackets are pretty obvious but screws and nails can be quite well disguised – they may just be covered with wax or filler, but could have a plug or patch over them, so a good visual inspection, combined with the use of a small metal detector, should find most of the foreign bodies.

Something else that is often found under upholstery is glue-soaked hessian wrapped around the front seat rail joints – and be warned, you will rarely find a pleasant surprise under hessian-encased joints!

Dismantling

Once all the metalwork and other debris has been removed it is time to persuade the joints to come apart. Some will quite literally fall apart, but sod's law being what it is, one or two joints will seemingly need a combination of Geoff Capes and Semtex.

As with any dismantling, it is a good idea to mark the joints using masking tape before starting so that all the bits go back in the right places. If the joints are hanging on tight, drill into the joint along the cheek of the tenon and introduce some hot water with a syringe. Sustained pressure on the joint is the safest way to persuade joints to separate. The Record 13½ reversible head cramp is excellent for dismantling chairs but sadly is no longer produced - there are, however, other cramps around which can be reversed. Alternatively, if the joint will come apart a little, softwood wedges with a shallow angle can be introduced at appropriate spots and

can help to keep the blood pressure down during this operation!

The setting out and angling of the mortices may be taken from any surviving bits of the mortice and tenon, or perhaps the other leg.

Tenons

The other element of the joint that often requires attention is the tenon. It may be worm damaged, metalwork damaged, or it may have parted company during the dismantling process! Either way, a false tenon will be needed but, once again, it is important to leave original surfaces undisturbed if at all possible.

tapped in gently with a pin hammer. If the joint just will not come apart it may be that the cramping pressure is being applied to only one side of the joint, making the tenon twist and lock within the mortice, or it may be that there is still some metalwork lurking within! Patience and persistence will ultimately get any joint apart – although if someone has used one of those nasty irreversible modern glues it could take some time!

Down to work

The tops of the front legs of the chair I have been working on recently virtually disintegrated, and to make a repair that will last requires the splicing on of some new wood. As with any splice, it must be long to be strong – but if done well, strength

will not be compromised.

On antique furniture, splices should be done in a way that will preserve as much as possible of the original surfaces – but a splice, by definition, is going to remove a big chunk of wood from somewhere! With this in mind, the splice is started at the highest point possible on the outside corner of the leg and finishes at a point much lower down on the inside corner of the leg. The mating surfaces will look diamond-shaped, if you've got it right, and result in the least possible amount of original surface being lost from the two outside faces which are the most visible. Gluing the splice can be a bit of a challenge because cramping will make the two pieces slide apart – this movement is restrained with a sash cramp. Another pair of hands

GLUES

I recently had a discussion with another restorer who suggested that all repair work to antique furniture should be carried out using Scotch glue – the idea being that all work should be reversible. As you can see from my previous articles, I am happy to use modern glues where they are appropriate, and a splice is a case in point. I can't really imagine why anyone would want a splice to the top of a leg reversed, but if you did, you could do it with the careful use of a bandsaw! So, for a leg splice, I would be happy to use Scotch glue as it is an excellent adhesive, but I would be equally happy to use a polyurethane glue such as Balcotan, which is incredibly strong and has a longer open time, which will make the gluing process far more relaxed.

"On antique furniture, splices should be done in a way that will preserve as much as possible of the original surfaces – but a splice, by definition, is going to remove a big chunk of wood from somewhere!"

A completed splice repair

On a seat rail for a stuff-over seat the top and outside surfaces will be covered with upholstery, whilst the other two surfaces may sometimes be seen. The new tenon in this case is therefore inserted from the top – but for a drop-in seat rail the tenon would normally be inserted from the underside, as the top surface will be visible and polished.

Completion

Having extended lines of the tenon's cheeks back from the shoulder to a length of approximately twice the height of the tenon, a saw cut is made down both lines to the depth of tenon and the waste removed with a chisel. Using a sliding bevel, the angle of the housing is transferred to the piece of wood, of the right species, that is being used for the new tenon and, having made the tenon/housing a snug fit, it is glued and cramped.

Once all necessary repair work has been completed the chair can be re-glued, using Scotch glue, and the repairs blended. ■

"Patience and persistence will ultimately get any joint apart – although if someone has used one of those nasty irreversible modern glues it could take some time!"

POTTED HISTORY

The early chairs of the Middle Ages could happily take all sorts of abuse being huge throne-like structures which were reserved for the head of the household who used his chair as a symbol of authority and superiority.

In about 1500 the 'joyned' chair was introduced, which was really just a development of a box – three of the sides were extended, one forming the back, with the other two extending to a lesser degree, to form the arms. They were decorated with carving which included such things as linenfold panels. These chairs were made from great thick lumps of oak and were so heavy that moving them was a challenge.

Chair design moved on, and in the 17th century chairs were beginning to look more like the chairs we know today – the 'wainscot' chair was still a heavy construction, designed with the belt and braces approach. The 'box' had disappeared but stretchers were retained almost at floor level, and the back was solid.

When Charles II returned to the throne in 1660 he brought with him craftsmen from the continent who preferred to work in the walnut that they were familiar with, and chair design succumbed to their influence, with their ornate carving, high backs and light caned panels – chairs became real fashion items.

In the early 18th century some daring chap decided to do away with the stretchers which I think made the cabriole legs of the time look much happier.

This was of course the thin end of the wedge and in contrast to the substantial chairs of the 15th century, the designers of the 2nd half of the 18th century were trying to see how little wood could be used whilst still producing a structure that could support the human form – perching delicately was a precarious enough occupation on some of these creations, anything remotely athletic would be a very short lived and somewhat dangerous occupation.

During dismantling, the tenon can break away completely

A new tenon is inserted from underneath to avoid it being visible - note the length for extra strength

When people think of 18th century furniture designers and makers, the names that trip off their tongues tend to be those of Chippendale, Sheraton, Hepplewhite and the like – they may have heard of Gillows but don't necessarily link the name with fine Georgian furniture.

The problem with Gillows is possibly caused by the fact that the firm was still in business in the 20th century, and the company was therefore far more

Ingenious cabinet maker

enduring than Chippendale and Co. But it had the effect of giving the name 20th century connotations which don't sit happily with the idea of fine antique furniture.

Leaving their mark

18th century English makers would often put their name to their furniture using a printed label but Gillows added their name with the recognised French method and stamped Gillows or Gillows of Lancaster somewhere discreet like the top edge of a door or drawer. To avoid confusion with the company's modern day production it is said that some 20th century dealers removed the stamped marks.

But fashions change and perhaps the furniture-buying public become more educated or discerning – we live in hope anyway – and now Gillows' furniture is

very sought after and people actively look for the stamped marks – if I were a sad, cynical furniture restorer I might suggest that it would be easy for someone to have a stamp made up to enhance furniture and capitalise on the punters' current desires – and if I were a sad, cynical furniture restorer I would also advise people to buy antique furniture from a dealer with a good reputation! ➤

The unusual and delicate feet

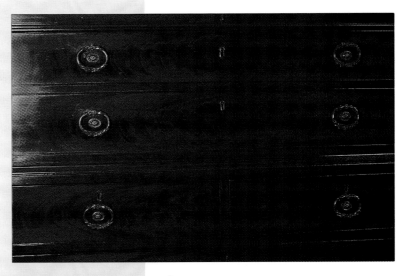

The quality of the veneers is superb

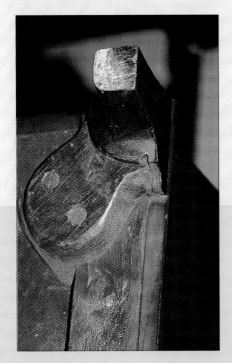

Construction of foot

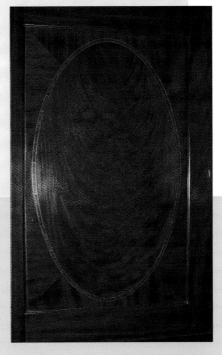

More of the stunning veneer on the doors

"It's a bit like looking at a very elegant Sumo wrestler who's made the unlikely switch to ballet and has been caught doing a little point work"

Robert Gillow

➤ Robert Gillow set up his workshop in Lancaster around 1730 and although his furniture was not at the cutting edge of design, lacking the refinement of London work, it was known for being well made, and always from the finest timber.

He must have been doing something right because by 1765 he had set up a shop in Oxford Street. A clue to his successful formula is to be found in a letter from a Mr Thomas Pennant who, in 1776, wrote that the firm of Gillows were "ingenious cabinet makers…who fabricate most excellent and neat goods at remarkably cheap rates" – this formula of high quality, no twiddly bits, and low cost, made Gillows the most successful manufacturers of the period.

Gillow's other claim to fame is that at the end of the 18th century he was commissioned to make some 'small desks' for a certain Captain Davenport – it could just be a coincidence but this might be the origin of the 'Davenport' desk?

Gillows' linen chest

I am rambling on about Gillows' furniture because I have recently had a piece in my workshop. The design is a little unusual in that it consists of a chest of drawers with a cupboard above containing shallow drawers. This layout would normally be referred to as a 'linen press', but the odd bit is the addition of a secretaire drawer between the chest and the cupboard. As we already know, Gillows' furniture is well made, and therefore, apart from any physical abuse that it might have endured at the hands of some human, and general wear and tear, we wouldn't expect to find too much wrong with it. This was pretty much the case apart from the secretaire drawer – its bottom was sagging, probably due to timber movement or lack of mid support – either way, the result was that it was pretty much jammed in the carcass and the internal fitments of the drawer were flapping about. Having persuaded the drawer to part company with the rest of the piece it was a relatively simple operation to flatten it and get it to work in the way to which it used to be accustomed.

Unusual features

As we also know, the design of Gillows' furniture is restrained, but there are some unusual features in this

The secretaire drawer displays equally fine work

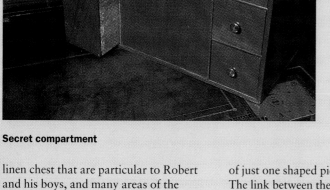

Secret compartment

More restrained and subtle work on the cornice

linen chest that are particular to Robert and his boys, and many areas of the construction that bring the word 'quality' to mind.

It is a large piece of furniture which I and my back can assure you is weighty, but when you look at what is supporting this great bulk you don't see the usual chunky bracket feet but incredibly delicate feet – it's a bit like looking at a very elegant Sumo wrestler who's made the unlikely switch to ballet and has been caught doing a little point work.

The construction of the feet is also unlike bracket feet. Rather than being made up of shaped pieces held together with glue blocks, each foot is made up

of just one shaped piece of mahogany. The link between the foot and the cabinet is made of a substantial piece of oak, which is housed into the top of the foot and is, in turn, secured to the underside of the cabinet using several substantial screws.

Craftsmanship

There is nothing unusual about the drawers in the lower half of the cabinet – flat fronts and cock beading being fairly standard – but the quality of the halved veneer is obvious, and the use of consecutive leaves has a stunning effect. This quality is repeated in the doors to the cabinet, which are a wonderful

flame veneer in an elliptical panel enhanced with a lighter inlay – with no visible gaps, glue lines or knife marks, just consummate craftsmanship.

Secret compartment

Inside the secretaire drawer, where some makers would let themselves get carried away, the restrained quality continues and, as with most secretaire drawers, there are secret compartments. It seems unlikely that any secret compartments were ever very secure, but they were an opportunity for the cabinetmaker to show us what he was made of.

Often these 'secret' bits will just ➤

Glue blocks on the cornice

Gilded handles are unique to Gillows

"It seems unlikely that any secret compartments were ever very secure, but they were an opportunity for the cabinetmaker to show us what he was made of"

➤ consist of hollow removable columns either side of the central door but on this piece there is a sprung wooden catch in the roof of the little cupboard which, when released, allows the whole central section – cupboard and flanking columns – to be drawn forward. The 'secret' bits are then accessed from the rear of this unit and consist of several small drawers which are housed in the space behind the columns. The columns are beautifully made with delicate vertical fluting and lovely crisp miniature mouldings top and bottom. The two outer columns are not just decorative, they overhang the side of the unit slightly and serve to cover the gap between unit and housing. If you didn't know it was there, you wouldn't know it was there – but I am sure that any self-respecting Georgian villain would gain access to your secret bits with the same alacrity that villains of today gain access to your Cortina.

Drawer

Behind the doors of the top cabinet are the shallow drawers that are always found in a linen press. Presumably the secretaire drawer was included so that you could rattle off a letter or two whilst choosing your duvet cover.

A nice touch in the design of the press drawers is the way that their oak bottoms extend a little way beyond the drawer sides – these extensions then run in grooves in the sides of the cabinet. Simple and effective and showing very little sign of wear.

Cornice

The crowning glory of any piece of furniture of this type is the cornice but, once again, Mr Gillow shows restraint – the moulding is relatively simple in design but nicely executed, and the dentils are crisp and perfectly spaced.

Cornices are very often removable but this one is firmly fixed, using the sort of technology I love, but that sadly is not an option for most people today because they use modern glues. The technology in question is the glue block – in this case the blocks are gargantuan but, as I am sure Stephen Fry once said, 'size doesn't matter'. If you are not familiar

with this high-tech jointing solution it consists of the formidable combination of bits of wood and pearl glue. You need to make sure that the surfaces of the glue blocks mate nicely with the surfaces being joined, add pearl glue to all surfaces, position the glue block, rub into position and leave to set. No cramps, no screws, no metal brackets, no stress, just sticky fingers!

Handles

The final embellishment to this lovely piece of furniture is the handles. The design is not the sort of thing you will find in any brassware catalogue and, as far as I am aware, is peculiar to Gillows' furniture. They are heavy cast ring handles, hinged at the top and embellished with leaves and flowers – and instead of the back plate that you would usually find on this sort of handle, there are separate central cast patera fitted to the drawer fronts with single cast spikes. As a final touch of class, all the handles, in fact every bit of brass on this piece, is gilt. Splendid! ■

Clever cures

I T IS REALLY quite remarkable how unobservant people are when looking at furniture. This is rather a depressing thought if you are a furniture designer-maker or a restorer who has just spent far too much time agonising over some tiny detail on your current project.

"So some bright spark came up with the idea of a drawer or two in the bottom of the chest and someone else came up with the rather uninspiring idea of naming the result a mule chest"

People come into my workshop with treasures they have just purchased at their local sale room which: "Just need a wax" – and you think to yourself, surely they must know that a chest of drawers should have four feet. At this point, in my case, I start to get a nasty nervous twitch as I think back to the time when I was training – we were given a role-playing exercise to teach us how to deal with clients when assessing a piece of damaged furniture to prepare an estimate. There were certain key questions that we were taught to ask and, as highly-trained experts in all things relevant to fine antique furniture, we were expected to be able to identify the smallest fault, the probable age of the piece, and whether it was fitted with all the right bits. Having survived the ordeal with the 'client', we all thought we had done rather well until some clever-dick started talking about what the design of the

LEFT: 18th century chest on chest needed repairs to its feet — many similar pieces have the same kind of problems

"This development meant that the joiner evolved into something of a prima donna and was called a cabinetmaker"

feet should have been – which was rather critical for this particular piece of furniture because all four feet were missing! Mind you, it wasn't a wasted exercise, and ever since that embarrassing incident I have developed a rather worrying furniture foot fetish.

Drawers and feet
The earliest chests or trunks had no feet and no drawers. The design of the chest developed from being a hollowed-out tree trunk to being framed and panelled with stile feet. Less wood was used, which resulted in a much lighter piece of furniture

RIGHT: This front
bracket foot was
the wrong shape,
length, and timber
– so it had to go

BELOW LEFT:
Having decided
to replace the
front feet, the
back needed the
same treatment

BELOW RIGHT:
New pine foot in
place with mitre
support block –
all held together
with Scotch glue

— which is important if you have to keep moving it between your various castles.

By the middle of the 17th century people were obviously getting mighty sick of never being able to find their William & Mary widgets which always made their way to the very bottom of the chest under their other treasures. So some bright spark came up with the idea of a drawer or two in the bottom of the chest and someone else came up with the rather uninspiring idea of naming the result a mule chest. It was then, of course, only a matter of time before someone decided that drawers from top to bottom would be a wonderful idea – any item you wished to find would be instantly retrievable, if only you could remember which drawer you had put it in.

This development meant that the joiner evolved into something of a prima donna and was called a cabinetmaker. So at the end of the 17th century chests of drawers were made in oak and walnut and were fitted with turned bun feet. By the middle of the 18th century chests of drawers were generally in mahogany and now had bracket feet which were often fairly square in design, but were also made in the ogee form. To make the bracket foot lighter and a little more delicate, the splayed bracket foot developed, becoming popular on Regency bow-front chests of drawers.

So, when confronted with a chest of drawers in an auction house, check that it has feet!

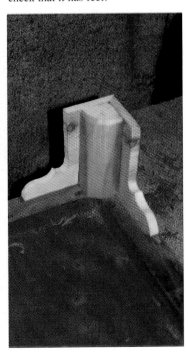

"If the chest is fitted with bracket feet and also has holes in its base, it is fairly safe to assume that it should be fitted with buns!"

Buns and brackets

Of course nothing is that simple – it may be fitted with feet but they may be the wrong design for the piece. It is always a good idea to take out the bottom drawer and check inside the base for holes which are an inch or so in diameter – if the chest is fitted with bracket feet and also has holes in its base, it is fairly safe to assume that it should be fitted with buns!

If you have a lathe, the necessary know-how, and some pictures to work from, replacing buns is relatively straightforward. If however, you don't have a lathe, the idea of replacing tired or missing buns with bracket feet must be a very appealing one, and just that has happened all too often over the years.

The anatomy of a bracket foot is a very simple one – no screws or nails are required in its construction nor should they be necessary in their repair! A foot consists of two pieces cut to the required shape with mitres cut at the corner – there is a fairly chunky piece which is fitted vertically in the corner and joins the two halves of the foot together, and there are two or more further pieces which join the top edge of the foot to the underside of the carcass.

ABOVE LEFT: More support blocks glued in place for the join between carcass and top edge of the foot

ABOVE: The rear foot given the same remedy – note the housing joint and simple angled rear piece, which will be against the wall

LEFT: Finished front foot veneered in burr elm

"A little light hammer veneering and some glue blocks is all that was needed to create something that looked a little more at home"

The technology used in the joining of all these various bits together is the rub joint – no metal needs to be introduced and no cramping is required, the only thing you need is some sticky stuff, and for this type of joint only Scotch sticky stuff will do. As with hammering veneer, the reason that it works is that the glue tacks quickly, but for it to work well the surfaces that are being jointed must be a good fit.

Rub joints

Rub joints are not, of course, just used to stick feet together. Any two pieces of wood, within reason, can be jointed with a rub joint – table tops for example. If you get a kick from low level technology this joint is for you.

Having prepared the two mating surfaces and achieved just the right viscosity with your glue, the two mating surfaces are coated with glue, placed together and rubbed against each other until you feel the glue just beginning to grab. Then you stop, preferably with the two pieces in their preferred final resting position, and you let go. Having said that you require no cramps at all, the odd bit of masking tape around the outside edge of the mitre joint can make life a little easier while the corner glue block is being rubbed into place.

Replacement feet

The chest we are working on here is in fact a chest on chest which had had its feet replaced at some point. The replacements were not really the right design, were not symmetrical, and were of different lengths. Also, they were in mahogany, and the rest of it was in walnut and burr elm – so the decision was made to replace them.

A template was needed to ensure that all the feet looked vaguely the same. These particular ones are in pine with a burr elm veneer to match the veneer of the drawer fronts. A little light hammer veneering and some glue blocks is all that was needed to create something that looked a little more at home. ■

DRAWER REPAIR

One of the drawer sides of the chest on chest was disintegrating. To rectify this, triangular pieces of oak were let in and then hand crafted to match the sockets. The pitch of the sides of the triangles is about the same as the final dovetails, just a little oversized to allow for trimming to fit.

To blend the backs of the new feet required some pigmented size and water stain – the dovetail repairs and the front faces of the new feet required a combination of chemical and cosmetic colouring to get them to blend.

ABOVE: Taken from the drawer side, three of the four dovetails needed replacing
BELOW: Oak spliced in slightly oversized to allow for final fitting

BELOW: A badly disintegrating drawer side required some major splicing

Cramping your style

Balloon back chairs from the Victorian era are one of the most awkward of shapes to cramp – blocks, bar, nuts and washers can be made into useful cramping devices

"A spindly chair loaded down with half a dozen sash cramps is not at all a happy chair"

There are several annoying adages in the world of woodworking – some just state the obvious and some are inaccurate. One saying which is both these is 'You can never have too many cramps!' It is, I suppose, a fairly sound sentiment, but a fine Sheraton chair would probably be able to put forward a fairly convincing argument to the contrary – a spindly chair loaded down with half a dozen sash cramps is not at all a happy chair.

Disappearing cramps

Another saying that is often heard in a woodworking workshop is 'Who's got all the cramps?' So, in essence, it's true, you can't have too many cramps – and if you've got loads of them they do look very inspiring if they are all hanging in neat rows on the wall, but one minute you'll look at those racks

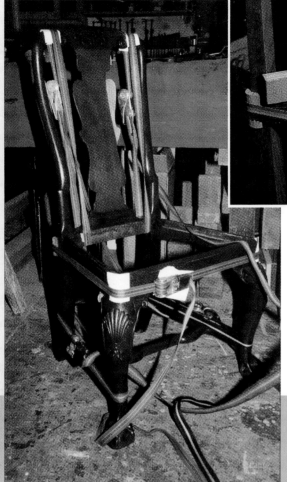

Band cramps to the rescue – these are simple devices but often offer the best solution for chair cramping

To avoid chairs that weren't designed to rock, from rocking, diagonal bracing cramped across the seat frame will help

"An open time of only a couple of minutes concentrates the mind wonderfully, encouraging meticulous planning of cramping operations"

and there are dozens of the things, the next minute when you've decided to glue-up a breakfront bookcase, they've all disappeared. Very worrying if you work on your own but a normal state of affairs if you share your workshop with others!

Kiss

Whether making or restoring, there will always be cramping challenges and I would suggest that these challenges come with greater regularity for a restorer than a maker, but they usually require not more and more cramps but a little ingenuity and the keeping in mind at all times of that acronym that you come across on management training courses: KISS – Keep It Simple Stupid! Very annoying but eminently sensible, and it seems to have etched itself indelibly on my brain.

Cramping arsenal

My cramping arsenal is the usual array of G-cramps, F-cramps and sash cramps but also has a lot of home-made cramping devices which includes long-reach cramps, modified upholstery springs, bicycle inner tubes, wind-surfer straps, old Victorian irons, odd-shaped bits of wood and wedges of varying shapes and sizes.

These items not only increase the size of your cramping capability, they also give you more flexibility – and happily most of them cost little or nothing!

Basic cramping

Basic cramping rules include the use of softening blocks at all times – original surfaces on antique furniture are never improved by the addition of cramp-shaped embossing, and that includes the surfaces that aren't seen – cramp

imprints on the underside of table tops and the insides of seat rails don't conjure up the word 'craftsmanship'.

Using a block which is not much bigger than the end of the cramp will give you plenty of pressure at that point but it will not do much softening and will just change the shape of the imprint! If there's glue around the cramping site, to avoid embarrassment, add some silicone baking paper or something similar between the block and the furniture, and don't view tightening cramps as an opportunity to exhibit muscular prowess. If a joint needs a huge amount of pressure to get it together there is a problem, and you're only kidding yourself if you think a cramp is going to solve it on a long-term basis, unless of course you plan to deliver the furniture with the cramps attached!

To add to the excitement of being a restorer, animal glue is used exclusively when gluing joints – an open time of only a couple of minutes concentrates the mind wonderfully, encouraging meticulous planning of cramping

> *"Dull and predictable perhaps, but I have no wish to have a coronary whilst gluing-up – although it would bring new meaning to the saying 'He came to a sticky end!'"*

Specially made blocks with rounded corners avoid cramping marks and allow the band to pull up

Blocks with extra bits to prevent slipping

operations, and is likely to keep you on good terms with those extra pairs of hands in the workshop.

Dry run

Doing a dry run is seen by some macho restorer types as a complete waste of time but I find the prizing apart of a half-glued item and the cleaning up of glue-coated joints even more of a waste of time.

I always do a dry run, and I then know that I have all the necessary cramps to hand, they are set to the right opening, and I have the opportunity of getting all the pieces laid out in the right place which means that the right tenon is likely to end up in the right mortice. Dull and predictable perhaps, but I have no wish to have a coronary whilst gluing-up – although it would bring new meaning to the saying 'He came to a sticky end!'

Difficult situations

The cramping situations that are going to require ingenuity are usually the ones that are an odd shape, in the middle of a large surface, or are just hard to get at. Chairs are a case in point as they are often an odd shape – the front seat rail is longer than the back seat rail, and the back, especially the cresting rail, can have some very interesting compound curves.

To deal with the cramping-up of a chair's seat rails is not too much of a problem if you glue-up the back and the front rails separately, but joining them together with the side rails can be a problem if you are using sash cramps, and sash cramps cannot be used at all if the seat frame is curved. The answer is to use band cramps – these put little strain on a chair's frame and are good at going round corners – they also give you the opportunity to glue-up the whole frame in one go, if you're feeling brave!

Band cramps

Softening still has to be considered where the band goes round the legs' outside edges and I solve this by the addition of some home-made corner blocks – I cut something close to a right angle on the inside face and round off the outside face to allow the band to slip round easily during tightening. To embellish this design, add little hats to the top of the front blocks to stop them sliding down the legs whilst getting the band on.

Often a band cramp is all that is needed to pull the joints up tight, but I always have a sash cramp to hand – if a joint does not immediately go up with the band, fit the sash cramp over the corner blocks and tighten as necessary. The tension on the band cramp will be sufficient to hold the frame in position, so the sash cramp can then be removed. ➤

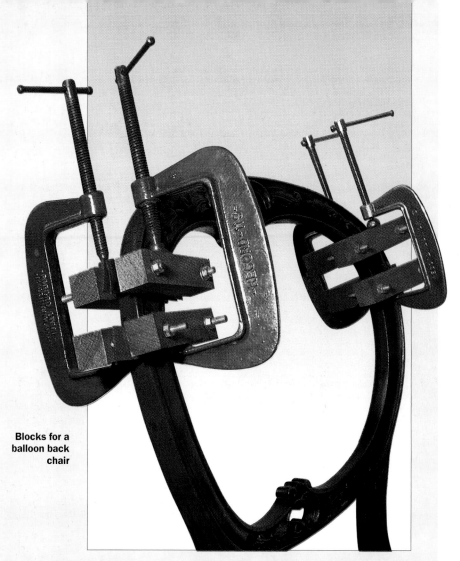

Blocks for a
balloon back
chair

Various cramping devices

De-wobbling

➤ I have found that clients are always more impressed if their chairs don't rock about when sitting on a flat floor. To achieve this happy situation I use two relatively substantial lengths of wood, a cramp, and something I know to be flat, such as the saw table. I place the chair on the table and if it wobbles I place the lengths of wood diagonally across the seat frame, one above and one below the rails, and the cramp is then added where the two pieces cross in the middle. It is critical which one goes above and which goes below otherwise the problem will only get worse – the one on the top must go over the legs that are high, as the effect of the cramping will then force the high legs down and the other legs up. You of course have a fifty-fifty chance of getting it right without even thinking about it, and if it's wrong it's fairly obvious what must be done to rectify the situation!

Curvy back

When chairs are made with a funny-shaped back, the maker will leave some flats in appropriate places to allow for cramping, and when glued, he will do the final shaping which will remove the flats. This is fine until the chair needs re-gluing when there will be nowhere sensible to put the cramps. Sometimes this can be overcome with the use of band cramps going over the cresting rail and around the rear seat rail, but even this arrangement is unlikely to result in pressure exactly where it is needed. The most severe case of a curvy back is perhaps the balloon back which was very popular in Victorian times and the only successful way I have found of cramping these is to make up some cramping flats that can be attached to the chair whilst cramping and then removed. The design I use is simple but effective, and consists of some short lengths of wood which are made into pairs and are held together with some threaded bar, nuts and washers.

The idea is to sandwich the chair back with each pair – the inside faces need to be roughly carved to the profile of the bit of chair they are to be fixed around, and a piece of inner tube can be added to give both a softening and non-slip effect, and to secure them the nuts are tightened. One pair is fitted just above the joint, one pair below, and small G-cramps are then positioned across each pair to the front and rear – this arrangement gives a cramping effect very close to the joint and also gives the opportunity to adjust the amount of pressure being applied to the front and rear to ensure that everything is in register.

Stress

The stress that can be induced in an otherwise laid-back restorer by the rather short open time that is experienced with animal glue can be reduced slightly by gently heating all the joints with a hot air gun before gluing, and always working in a nice warm workshop! Also, a form of animal glue called Sheppy Tug, which has formaldehyde in it, has a slightly longer open time than pearl glue, but warm workshops and formaldehyde will not save you from the perils of not planning your cramping! ▪

Restorer with cramp

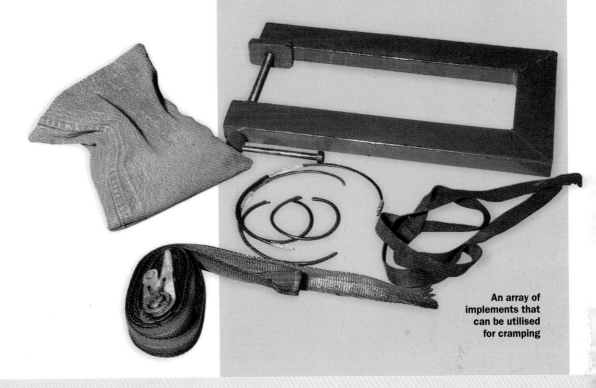

An array of
implements that
can be utilised
for cramping

Having covered the basic cramping rules and the cramping-up of a piece of oddly-shaped furniture in the previous chapter, I am now tackling some of the other cramping challenges that regularly come a restorer's way. Cramping can easily end up giving you one of those tense headaches that make you wish you'd listened to your careers master at school and become an accountant. As I mentioned before, the key to success is often just to keep the whole thing as simple as possible – if you catch yourself staggering across the workshop loaded down with ropes, pulleys, hydraulic jacks and scaffolding, there is just a chance that you haven't hit upon the best solution!

Awkward places

Applying pressure to the middle of a large surface such as a table top can, on the face of it, be a bit of a problem as,

with the best will in the world, a G-cramp will only reach a few inches in from the edge of anything. However, a pair of G-cramps can be used to get to the middle of a large surface if combined with a block of MDF – not too small – and a couple of sturdy wooden bars that reach from one side of the table to the other.

The MDF block is positioned over the bit that needs cramping, one bar is balanced on top of the block, the other is put under the table, the cramps are then fitted across the ends of the bars and tightened to give the required pressure. If you are able to manage this arrangement with one pair of hands, you're wasted in a workshop and should consider a career in a circus as a contortionist.

The bar under the table is important as it gives support under the area being cramped – if it is omitted you will probably need to move swiftly to an

"If you catch yourself staggering across the workshop loaded down with ropes, pulleys, hydraulic jacks and scaffolding, there is just a chance that you haven't hit upon the best solution!"

article which covers jointing broken table tops and panels!

Custom made

If you find that you are not a budding circus performer and have no friends in your workshop, there are other things

> *"If you are able to manage this arrangement with one pair of hands, you're wasted in a workshop and should consider a career in a circus as a contortionist."*

➤ that can be tried. If the bits that require the cramping are not too far from the edge, you could pay your local blacksmith a visit and get him to make up some long reach cramps out of some box-section tubing and threaded rod. These are relatively light and give a good degree of control, but to be effective and not too unwieldy, will only reach somewhere between 300 to 460mm (12 to18in).

Other technology

If the area you need to get to is right in the middle of something extremely wide, and it usually will be, musical instrument making technology could be brought to bear. Lengths of springy wood known as 'go-bars' are used for pressing the sound-board of a piano, and this method can be used for general cramping if your workshop has a substantial beam or joist to push against. The work-piece must be well supported under the beam on a substantial table or trestles and the go-bars must have a length which is a little greater than the distance between the work-piece and the beam, the bars are then bent to enable them to fit under the beam – the longer the bar, the greater the pressure.

Mini go-bar technology can be used to great effect within the confines of a carcass for such things as drawer runner repairs. A variation on this theme is to use a sash cramp in place of the go-bar – I usually have the end with the threaded adjuster sitting in a little indentation in the top of a softening block and the other end against the beam. This system gives precise control of the amount of pressure being applied – but to avoid that sickening crash or crunching noise of a falling sash cramp against an antique surface, secure the top end to the beam with a piece of string!

If all this is far too high-tech and all that is required is a little pressure to hold down a piece of veneer whilst it is gluing, stick something heavy on it such as an old Victorian iron or an old imperial measuring weight that is no longer acceptable to those enlightened chaps at the European Commission.

Banding

To hold a piece of veneer banding, stringing or narrow moulding to the edge of something would be a little tricky if it were not for masking tape. Stretching the tape to the point where it is just about to

RIGHT **Masking tape can be effective – but be careful it doesn't take off the finish with it**

BELOW **Mini go-bars being used to cramp a drawer runner repair**

"Old inner tubes make wonderful cramps and can get you out of many a jam – they are also free, unless you don't know anyone with a bicycle"

break, before sticking it down, will give a little pressure and sticking two bits together to double the thickness will allow even more pressure to be applied. Very simple, but not without its drawbacks because when it is removed it may remove with it some of the original polished surface, so I always test the surface I am to stick tape to for durability and if it is a little fragile, I don't leave the tape on for too long.

Inner tubes

Old inner tubes make wonderful cramps and can get you out of many a jam – they are also free, unless you don't know anyone with a bicycle. The tube is just cut into strips of various lengths, the wider the strip, the greater the pressure

that can be applied. They are particularly useful for holding oddly-shaped or curved pieces together, they are light, will grip most surfaces, even polished ones, but are soft so won't cause any damage.

In the event that the curve is too severe for the tube to grip, it may be possible to put a cramp of some sort onto the curved surface and then use that cramp as an anchor point around which to wind the tube.

Spring cramp

Another 'free' cramp is the spring cramp which is made from an old upholstery spring. While it is not as versatile as the inner tube, it is light and useful for cramping things such as drawer runner repairs. A little time is

required to make them and the quickest way of cutting them to length is by using a bench grinder, which can also be used to form a point on the end if required.

The downside of these cramps is that the points may cause a great deal of damage to the surface being cramped, so softening is definitely a consideration – they also have the habit of occasionally pinging across the workshop when you are least expecting it which might increase your heart rate for a minute or two and can caused damage, so be careful where they are aimed!

Shaped blocks

Such things as canted corner and curved drawer fronts may on first inspection seem a little tricky but these problems are usually overcome with the use of shaped blocks. To cramp the edge of a concave drawer front needs a block of the same shape as the front but also ➤

Inner tube utilised in the repair of an arm, with cramps used to give extra purchase

Spring clamps holding a drawer runner

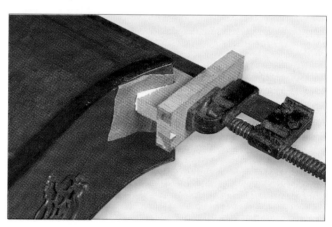

LEFT and ABOVE **Sash cramp holding canted corners**

➤ needs a 'hook' on it to prevent it from just sliding down the slope when pressure is applied with a sash cramp. Cramping a carcass with canted corners on the front is again achieved with the use of shaped blocks but this time a combination of sash cramps running at right angles to each other will have the effect of applying the pressure where it is needed, whilst also stopping them from slipping off.

Even pressure can be applied to a coopered column by using a band cramp in conjunction with a piece of 'bendy-ply' or kerfed MDF and, if necessary, any odd-shaped cramping situation can have the pressure spread more evenly by the introduction of some polystyrene under the softening blocks.

Sand bags

Sand bags are not just for the army and flood defenses, on a small scale they are very useful for cramping. I find that the best material for making the bag itself is denim and part of a leg from an old pair of jeans is perfect, as you just need to sew across the top and bottom to form a bag.

The sand can be heated, which is useful when using Scotch glue, and the bag will conform to almost any shape. I got a little carried away with the design of my first sand bag and persuaded my resident seamstress to sew a zip into one of the ends to allow me to remove the sand for heating – this is really quite unnecessary and I now leave the sand in the bag and put it straight onto an electric hot plate, on a low setting! Getting engrossed in something else while it is cooking is not to be advised though, the smell of burning denim is not a pleasant one and the arrival of the fire brigade can be a little distracting.

Sand bags are particularly useful for gluing veneer to compound curves such as can be found on the moulded edge of a circular table top, the weight of the bag will apply some cramping pressure but if this is not sufficient, weights or cramps can be added.

Appropriate system

Bear in mind that some of the above techniques will be able to give more cramping pressure than others – some will give little control and some will be too heavy or clumsy for a delicate piece of furniture. All of these things must be taken into account when choosing the appropriate system for a particular job and often a combination of techniques will be required, or they may need to be adapted for a particular situation. Generally, though, with a little thought they will solve most problems without needing to reach for the Anadin. ■

From buns to cabrioles

Chest on stand restored with original cabriole legs

It is the middle of the 17th century and chests have already come a long way from their original incarnation of a hollowed-out tree trunk which, in my opinion, was potentially much more fun if used as a boat rather than as a receptacle for your worldly goods, but that's just me!

So, the tree trunk has refined itself with the help of a pit saw and a little 'frame and panel' technology. It has even gained a few drawers in the base and maybe a removable tray in the top, but the next big step forward was the fitting of drawers from top to bottom.

The first examples were a sort of hybrid as they were, on the face of it, cabinets, but on opening the doors, drawers were revealed, a bit like the top part of a linen press.

Apart from the fact that having lots of drawers makes mornings a bit less of a challenge, because your socks can be separated from your doublets, the necessity for storing clothes in drawers rather than in chests was brought about by the restoration of Charles II to the throne. The way that furniture develops, due to the circumstances of the time, is the aspect that I think makes it so fascinating. Apart from the development of techniques and tools, it is very often the social requirements of a particular time that have brought about

changes in design, or the introduction of new items.

Fashion

The implication of Charles II being put on the throne was that there was a reaction by all the fashion victims of the day against the terribly dull Puritan rule of Cromwell and his cronies – a love of dress spread, and the relevance of this was that the fashionable items of the day, which were made from much thinner materials, would suffer if they were stored in a chest with no drawers. Imagine the effect of storing your new floaty designer numbers under half a hundredweight of other clothes. So ➤

Cabriole legs were used on a wide range of furniture, as on this Davenport desk

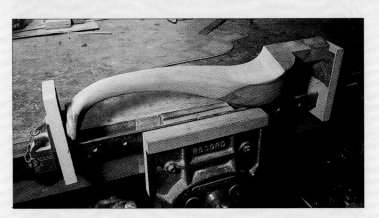

Cabriole leg in the making

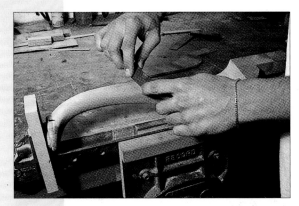

Spokeshaving by hand is a good method for final shaping

➤ lots of drawers were needed to keep designer numbers at their uncrushed best.

But, not content with having one's clothes kept in pristine condition in a chest of many drawers, in about 1685 stands were introduced for chests. This elevated the lower drawers from the ground which was of course much more convenient, and was a good preventative measure against the misery of lower back pain.

You can't really deny the practicality of raising your drawers to a more convenient and easily accessible height, but it does seem a little foolhardy to perch something heavy on something of a rather delicate construction. The earliest stands weren't too flimsy, because they consisted of six turned legs which were beefed up a bit by being all joined together with flat stretchers a little way off the ground. But later

versions were themselves fashion victims, and they dispensed with two of the legs and all the stretchers because a newer, sexier leg had arrived from the continent.

Cute cabriole

This new voluptuous innovation was the cabriole leg and it was introduced into English furniture in about 1700. These new legs were used extensively on chairs – think of the classic Queen Anne chair – and on stands, and they were so popular that they stayed in favour with furniture designers and makers until about 1780.

The only slight drawback with a cabriole leg is that its curvaceous design, that tapers to the visually pleasing slim ankle, makes it a rather fragile item. Combine this fragility with the loads that it has to endure when supporting a chest of drawers, and the fact that it was

made from walnut which is not the strongest of woods and is a favourite snack of the furniture beetle, and you will quickly come to realise why so many stands have lost their original legs.

Quick fix

The quick, easy way of dealing with damaged cabrioles on a stand is to throw the legs away and fit a set of bun feet in their place but this, as I am sure you will realise, will make the whole structure sit rather closer to the ground and, in my view, make it look rather strange and unbalanced. The other consequence of this rather misguided action is to make the top surface of the chest visible for all to see. This wouldn't be too much of a problem if the top were veneered, but why veneer the top of something when it can't be seen – remember that 18th century people

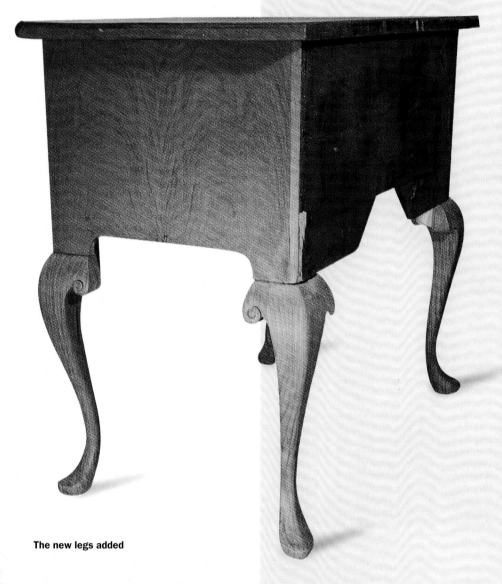

The new legs added

*"...they dispensed
with two of the legs
and all the stretchers
because a newer,
sexier leg had arrived
from the continent"*

Detail of new leg

were fitted with much shorter legs than we are today (well most of us anyway).

So, the quick fix for a chest on stand with broken legs in the past was to fit buns to the stand and veneer the top. One of my clients who possessed a chest on stand that had received just this treatment refused to entertain the idea of reinstating the original style of legs because it had been in the family like this for as long as she could remember, and to her it looked right!

Detective work

There are, however, people who want their stands to be reinstated to their original precarious design and far be it from me to try to dissuade them – quite apart from the fact that it's work, cabriole legs are very pleasing things to create.

The first thing to do when embarking on the re-creation of missing legs is to

decide upon the design, which usually involves a good deal of detective work and pouring over hundreds of pictures in furniture books and catalogues – once you start studying the cabriole form you will be amazed at the huge variation in design.

Re-creating leg

Having decided on a shape that was both appropriate for the particular piece that I had in the workshop, and was acceptable to its owner, I made a full scale drawing of the new leg on a piece of thin ply. I then transferred the shape from the template to two adjacent faces on an appropriately-sized, square-sectioned piece of walnut – the orientation being that the 'knees' touch on the arris of the blank.

The plan was then to cut the blank to the rough cabriole shape on the bandsaw. Following the shapes drawn

on the first face is straightforward enough, but when you come to do the second cut at right angles to the first, you need a cunning plan – because you have just cut off your markings and the blank is no longer square, and no longer sits flat on the bandsaw table.

There are two approaches that can be adopted – I either stick the bits that have just been cut off back on with tape, or I cut just less than half way along the marked line from either end and leave a small 'bridge' in the middle of the cut which holds everything together whilst I cut from the other direction. I find that 'bridges' are quicker than faffing about with sticky tape, but it doesn't really make very much difference.

Shaping

Having cut the legs to their rough shape, the rest of the shaping is done with a spokeshave, a cabinet scraper, ➤

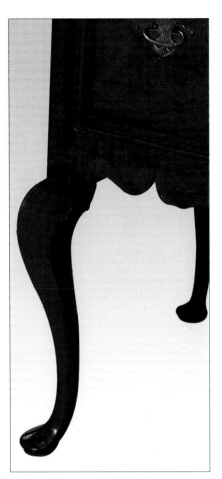

**Awaiting finish –
viewed from the front**

The polished leg

Finished stand

➤ and sand paper, in that order. But a cabriole leg is a tricky thing to hang on to whilst shaping, and my secret weapon is a sash cramp which is fitted with MDF pads, one at each end. The MDF pads have a rectangular slot cut in them on the morticer and they then fit snugly on the bar of the sash cramp and, with the addition of a piece of fairly coarse sandpaper stuck to the bit that makes contact with the leg, will hold the leg between them without slipping – and

the sash cramp, with the addition of some packing pieces can be held in the bench vice.

If you're a natural carver you will be able to do the rest of the shaping by eye and intuition but I find that I need a little guidance in the form of a few pencil lines.

Ankle

The critical part of the leg is the ankle, the narrowest part of the leg just

above the foot. The leg at this point is circular in cross section and, apart from the foot itself if it is a pad foot, is the only part that is. So, I roughly find the mid point between the arrises and, using my finger as a fence to keep this dimension, I extend this line either side of the ankle, running my finger along the arrises.

I do this twice on each face from each arris, and these lines then become the sacred lines that I don't want to remove – all the wood that is required to be removed is between these lines. Additional lines can be added but they can just confuse matters and, if the shaping is done systematically, it really isn't that difficult to get a very good result.

The bit that makes it all a little more tricky is when there is carving on the knees, or the foot is a 'ball and claw', but that sort of embellishment is usually reserved for cabrioles on chairs, thankfully! ■

This Pembroke table suffered from the
attentions of a feline 'sculptor'

Cat scratch fever

There are many things which can conspire to injure an innocent piece of antique furniture... A beetle may decide your chair's seat rails are a perfect place in which to bring up a large family; one of those firms of 'careful' movers may regress into a firm of 'not so careful because we're in a bit of a rush' movers. You may have been rather careless and introduced some 'little people' into your home and omitted to put your treasures into storage until they had been persuaded to leave home. Or you may have been walking in the vicinity of a pet shop when, for some inexplicable reason, were momentarily caught off your guard by a small, innocent looking bundle of fur and reached for your wallet, without even a moments thought for the frightening combination of razor sharp claws and equally sharp feline wit that'll effortlessly spot

the similarity between a scratching post and the legs of your antiques!

Gentle creatures?

We all know pets can be destructive, and it can be most annoying to get all dressed up to go jogging and find you no longer possess two running shoes! But losing a running shoe is not going to be the end of the world, you can either pursue the concept of 'hopping for health' or you have the option of buying some more shoes at some point and, in the meantime, have a few nights off relaxing in front of the television. Pet induced carnage directed towards your fine antiques is, however, something that can bring on a bout of serious, and rather longer lasting depression that may also have an undesirable effect on your bank balance. You would think this depression would be swiftly followed by the demise of

the perpetrator of the heinous crime, but us soppy pet owners seem to be more than a little soft in the head, and ridding ourselves of an evil four legged menace, just because it has reduced the value of a treasured antique by several thousand pounds, is a solution rarely considered.

Red in tooth and paw

In my time as a furniture restorer I've come across several cases of canine and feline induced damage, which tends to be in the form of chewed legs and scratched surfaces. Although I have to say one of the worst and definitely the most unpleasant cases I had the misfortune to deal with was the grisly case of the chiffonier plinth that a misguided tom had taken into its head to 'spray' on a regular basis. The softwood groundwork of the plinth was completely sodden and the smell

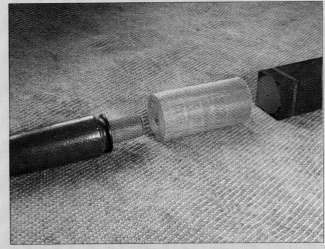

Left: The damage done

Top: Spigot and turned blank

Above: Glued together

was unbelievable, and to this day I don't know what on earth possessed me to take the job on, but if you ever find yourself faced with this sort of challenge, I strongly suggest you invest in a sturdy pair of Marigolds, a large can of air freshener, open all windows and work really fast!

The table I'm working on this month has suffered, not only from the rather selfish attentions of a cat with a good set of sharp claws, but also from the rather misguided attentions of the cat's owner who had a nice, sharp saw! The cat's attentions being directed at the tops of the turned legs and the damage consisting of vertical scratching which over a period of time had, in places, succeeded in removing most of the detail from the turnings. The owner's attentions being directed at the bottoms of the legs, with the simple aim being to make the table a bit lower so

it could be used for eating from whilst seated in a low chair. From the photos you'll see this is not one of the finest examples of a Pembroke table. A better one might be made from inlaid satinwood, the top could be oval or serpentine in shape and it would probably stand on elegant square tapered legs, but this table was of great sentimental value for its present owner who had inherited it from his father. As a boy he remembered it to be in fairly pristine condition and he was keen to get the table back into something close to its original height and condition.

Leg work

I decided the most appropriate way of dealing with the damage to the tops of the legs was to replace the most badly damaged sections, the extent of which varied from leg to leg. The general rule when repairing/replacing sec-

tions of damaged turnings is to position the join between the old and new bits at a place where you are unable to see the join. This invisible joint line is at a point where the turning makes a dramatic change of direction, namely in the valley between two consecutive convex turnings or perhaps at an internal angle where a flat shoulder changes to a convex shape. So, having decided where to make the incisions, the next point to consider is how to join the original and new bits together and the only way that really works is to turn spigots and drill holes on the ends of the various bits.

On this particular table, the leg/frame joints were all loose, which meant the whole table was going to be dismantled anyway for glueing. Having taken the table apart, I made the decision to put each leg in the lathe and turn one of the jointing spigots ➤

Spliced in new tenons

"In my time as a furniture restorer I've come across several cases of canine and feline induced damage which tends to be in the form of chewed legs and scratched surfaces"

New piece on the feet for bucket castors

Nasty 'blobby' things

➤ onto the leg itself, within the damaged turned sections. The plan was, therefore, to have a spigot turned onto the lower half of the leg which would locate into an appropriately sized hole in the new turned repair piece, this in turn would have a spigot turned onto its upper end which would fit into a hole in the top of the leg. The thinking behind this was that the spigots and sockets would be kept in the largest section of each leg, each leg tapers below the damaged areas, also the spigot, if turned onto the leg would automatically be at right angles to its shoulder, whereas drilling a perpendicular socket into the end of a tapering leg can be a bit of a challenge!

Spigots

The lack of height on this table was due to the fact the man with the saw had chopped off the original castors, thus losing about 50mm (2in) in the overall height of the table. To fit new bucket castors to regain this lost height meant first recreating the tapered spigots on which to fix the castors. I therefore turned up some extension pieces a little oversize and fitted them to the ends of the legs using a spigot and socket. The arrangement of mounting the legs onto the lathe to turn the spigot at the top end had the added benefit that the extensions at the foot of each leg could be easily turned to the required taper to fit the new castors. The only really critical part of this turning exercise was to make sure that the leg was mounted centrally at each end, and at the top end of the leg the centre marks of the original

The refurbished table, back as man intended

To shine, or not to shine?

To the finish

The drop handles fitted to the drawer fronts struck me as being rather nasty 'blobby' things, and having removed them to enable the wood to be repolished, it was obvious from the additional fixing hole they were neither original nor the right style. The original holes were in the centre of the backplates and it could be assumed the original handles were knobs, not drops. The client agreed to new handles which duly arrived looking rather splendid and very shiny; which leads me on to the question of how shiny brass fittings should be? The client in this case wanted the new fittings to be shiny, but not too shiny. Suppliers of new fittings vary in their approach to the coefficient of shine, some will only supply 'bright polished', some will offer the additional possibilities of 'fully antiqued' or 'highlighted' and suppliers to the repro trade will supply 'bright polished and lacquered' or 'antiqued' which involves the fittings being covered in an uneven coating of brown splodge, which to my eye looks a bit of a dog's breakfast.

So to achieve the 'not too shiny' look I ordered 'fully antiqued' fittings and brought them up to the required degree of shine with a piece of 0000 wire wool and some dark wax. If, however, I were unsure what 'fully antiqued' meant, perhaps from an unfamiliar supplier, I would order the fittings 'bright polished', dunk them in some stripper to remove any lacquer and then 'fume' them in ammonia, which has the effect of making the brass go dull. I would then use a combination of wax and 0000 wire wool to bring them back to the required level of shine! All of which may seem like a lot of effort for not much difference. I may seem a rather sad case, but to a lot of people, especially in the trade, it's these little details which make all the difference.

I often feel with antiques that have been restored, and even new pieces of furniture people have lovingly crafted, the fittings really don't do the piece justice and a little more attention to detail in this area would mean that the overall effect was not spoilt!

The right amount of shine

lathe used to turn the legs were still clearly visible and at the foot I just used a centre finder, and although a certain amount of luck might have been involved, it worked very well. It's fairly obvious all the spigots in this exercise were created on the lathe, one way or another, and it is also fairly obvious that the holes or sockets into which the spigots were fitted were created with a drill, but I would counsel you not to use just any old drill, but to invest in a saw tooth cutter if you wish your sockets to be accurate. The saw tooth cutter is very similar to a Forstner bit but is comfortable stuck into end grain, where it won't have any tendency to wander about while cutting.

Putting it back together

Having sorted out the legs, it was time to re-glue the table, but before this could be done I had to recreate a couple of tenons on one end of the dummy drawer front. Original surfaces of the visible kind are the most important to conserve, so I recreated the tenons from the unseen side, and I used a router to create the housings for the new tenons in both cases. The lower housing, I just tapered down to the lower edge at a nice shallow angle, and the top housing was parallel sided and terminated at the screw pocket. Although these repairs will not be visible when the table is standing in its usual position, unless you happen to be lying on the floor, it's still important for them to be as discreet as possible, and as part of the finishing process I coloured out these repairs as well as the more visible ones, and colouring out a repair with a nice shallow joint line or one that is hidden in the shadows of a screw pocket is relatively easy! ∎

When a grandfather is not a grandfather

There are various items of furniture that I have something of a soft spot for and one of them is the longcase clock. Now, you may think, as I once did, that a long wooden box standing on its end with a clock perched on top is called a grandfather clock but, in the world of antiques, if you were to utter the words 'grandfather clock' you might be given one of those supercilious looks that some antique dealers are so good at.

Naming

It's just one of those things – every profession or industry is the same – it's a bit like being in a club and having secret passwords and dubious handshakes. If you don't call things by the name that the club has deemed, in its wisdom, to be the right name, you aren't considered to be a

A rather bad previous repair

member and must therefore be a poor uneducated punter! So, a grandfather clock is a longcase clock and by the same token, a tall boy is a chest-on-chest. Read, learn and inwardly digest to avoid embarrassment and ridicule when you find yourself within the hallowed walls of an antique shop or sale room. Of course a longcase clock is a grandfather clock by any other name, and if you have ➤

LEFT **The capitals were falling apart and the moulding needed replacing on this longcase clock case**

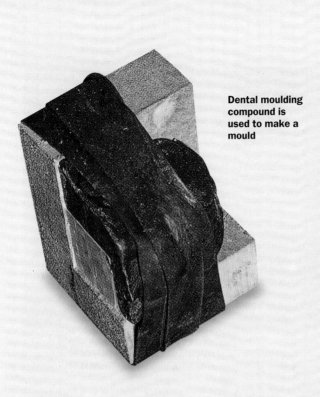

Dental moulding compound is used to make a mould

The finished capital

> *"Clocks were large, fixed, and driven by hanging weights until c1500 when some clever chap discovered a new motive power – a coiled spring in a drum"*

➤ money in your pocket and look as if you are willing to part with it, you could call it whatever you wanted!

History

Having decided to look at the longcase clock this month, I was prompted to research its history and see how and why it developed into its now familiar shape. It would seem that in medieval times clocks were around but they would have been public clocks, and in all probability had no dials or hands and just struck the hour. Now, if you had gone to all the trouble of making a clock that informed you that another hour had passed, it would seem sensible to know which hour it was, so that you knew how long it was till lunch-time. To achieve this level of sophistication in those days you would in all probability employ someone to strike a bell the requisite number of times by hand. Quite a pleasant job I suppose – plenty of free time interspersed by a little light bell ringing – although there could be an element of stress if you fell asleep and were woken on the hour by the clock in the sort of incoherent stupor that I find myself in every morning, not having the faintest idea what day it is, let alone the hour!

Horological breakthroughs

Clocks were large, fixed, and driven by hanging weights until c1500 when some clever chap discovered a new motive power – a coiled spring in a drum. This resulted in much smaller portable clocks with an hour dial and hand – at this point there was no wood involved as they were constructed entirely of metal – but their accuracy was affected by such things as the weather.

The next big horological breakthrough c1658 was the introduction of a pendulum as a regulato. Once again clocks were driven by weights, but this time they could run from eight days up to a year on a single winding.

A Londoner, with the rather unusual name of John Smith, then discovered that a long pendulum with a heavy weight and small swing kept much better time than a short one with a large swing. This, by a happy coincidence, fitted very neatly into a tall thin wooden case which also prevented the weights and pendulum from being fiddled with by inquisitive fingers. At this point, then, the clock gave the cabinetmaker another vehicle on which to show off his talents. Rare, beautifully figured woods were used, as was marquetry and parquetry often embellished with gilt carving and ormolu mounts – and so the longcase clock became an important, highly decorated piece of furniture.

Country clocks

Having just described longcase clocks from the top end of the market, it must be remembered that the less extravagant folk in the country also needed to know when it was tea-time. Pendulum technology was known about and used, which meant that a wooden case was still required but with rather more restrained decoration. The case on the particular clock I am working on this month is oak, and the only real decoration, apart from the use of mouldings, is the columns on the hood which have gilt capitals and plinths.

This scratch stock will not wander

Cutting the moulding

The missing moulding

"At this point a visit to my dentist was required, not because restoring longcase clocks gives me tooth-ache, but because this particular repair process needs dental moulding compound"

Repairs

Unfortunately, these small gilt embellishments were, in a couple of cases, disintegrating. One of the capitals – the bits at the top of the column – was obviously in a bad way and had taken on a rather blobby appearance due to some previous, uninspired repair work. The plinth – the bit at the bottom – of the same column didn't look too bad until it was touched, when it became obvious that the gilt outer skin was surrounding a lot of fresh air and a little white powder.

I therefore made the decision to replace the capital and the plinth on this column. Fortunately, the corresponding pieces on the column on the opposite side of the hood were sound, so I had something to copy. At this point a visit to my dentist was required, not because restoring longcase clocks gives me tooth-ache, but because this particular repair process needs dental moulding compound.

The plan was to make casts with the moulding compound, but the important thing here was to take the casts from the intact originals without damaging them. I gave the originals and the immediately

surrounding area a coating of clear wax and then gently pressed the compound into place and carefully removed it when it had hardened At this point I had the front halves of the moulds but required the backs. I simply made these from a couple of small pieces of MDF fixed at a right angle to each other and, having given the moulds' surfaces a coating of release agent wax, I fixed the two halves together with a strip of inner tube.

Gilding

The bits that I was replacing were made from a white powdery material which was probably plaster, but I made the decision to make the replacements from two-pack polyester filler which is quick and easy to use and doesn't shrink when it is curing.

The conservation watchword, as we all know, is 'reversibility' so, with this in mind, I fitted the new capital and plinth to their new homes with a reversible glue – pearl glue of course fills this criteria, Paraloid would also be a good choice, and the V&A apparently have a penchant for fish glue.

The finish on the originals was not in fact gilding, as in oil or water gilding, but was bronze paint which is a poor man's version, and consists of a metal powder in a vehicle such as shellac. Bottles of metallic paint can be purchased from art shops in various shades and, having 'gilded' the replacements with the appropriate colour paint, I toned them to blend with the originals.

Scratch-stock

A length of moulding was missing from the lower part of the case and because it is not really appropriate to set up a spindle moulder to make 254mm (10in) of moulding I decided to go low-tech and use a scratch-stock. As luck would have it, I had recently been to my dentist for some moulding compound which was just what I needed to create a cutter of the right profile.

I waxed a section of the remaining original moulding to prevent the compound from becoming a permanent feature, made a casting with the compound and transferred the profile to a piece of metal. Some people use ➤

Finished moulding

"Now, all self-respecting furniture restorers will possess a beautiful scratch-stock, usually crafted by their own fair hand – and I am no exception"

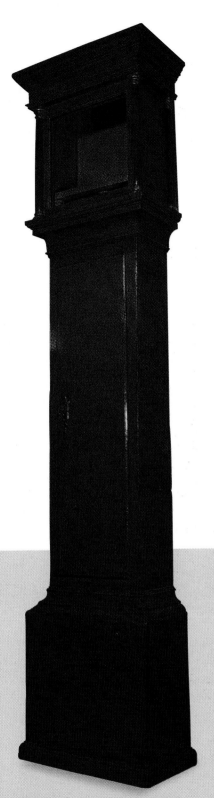

Restored and
cleaned and awaiting delivery

➤ white correcting fluid to mark onto, but I covered an area of the metal with marker pen and scribed the profile onto it with a fine spike. I used a combination of hacksaw and warding files to encourage the metal to take the profile of the scribed line and, having created the cutter, I just required the scratch-stock.

Now, all self-respecting furniture restorers will possess a beautiful scratch-stock, usually crafted by their own fair hand – and I am no exception. But when scratching a narrow moulding, especially in a hard wood such as oak, the cutter mounted in a scratch-stock of conventional design will try to wander about, and can give a rather wobbly-looking end result. To combat this tendency I usually make up a holder for the cutter with a slot cut in it where the cutter sits, and which snugly straddles the piece of wood from which the moulding is being made, thus stopping the wandering.

Sod's law being what it is, every moulding I have copied in the past has been a different width, so I have an ever-increasing number of slotted scratch-stocks – but this time one of the collection was a perfect fit and goes to prove that, as every restorer knows, you should never throw anything away!

A scratch-stock is a wonderfully simple bit of kit but using one, even one that can't wander about, requires practice, and is a question of feel and a little finesse. Quite apart from the versatility that it can give you, I find that you have a feeling of getting in touch with those 17th and 18th century cabinetmakers who didn't have the option of spindle moulders and routers – and they didn't have to wear ear defenders or miss the really interesting bits from Radio 4 either!

Finish

The finish was a major consideration on this clock-case as it was extensively covered with a dark gloop that detracted from the surrounding wood which was a lovely golden brown. I gave the whole case quite a severe clean to remove the gloop, and then coloured the new length of moulding to blend it to its new surroundings, and finally built up the surface with wax polish.

I have to say that I am convinced that a longcase clock would appreciably enhance the working environment of a furniture restorer's workshop, but this clock's owner seemed equally convinced that the enhancement of his hall was of greater importance – perhaps his resident bell-ringer had become unreliable and was being updated! ■

This refined rosewood sofa table revealed an elegant simplicity in its construction

Out of joint

There has recently been an exchange of views in the letters page of F&C which refers to carcass construction, types of joints and the use of biscuit joints. Whilst I don't want to directly join this debate, it did prompt me to think about modern jointing techniques, equipment and materials compared to the traditional variety.

MDF or not MDF?

As far as materials are concerned, and here I would certainly include the likes of MDF, I have heard more than one professional woodworker state with great confidence: "If MDF had been around in the 18th century, Chippendale would have used it!" And, I suppose, in all probability he would! On the downside, if he had used MDF there's a good chance I wouldn't be quite so busy as a restorer. To some extent my earning

a living as a restorer relies on the fact that wood moves, so with MDF on the scene I would have to rely more heavily on the valuable contributions made to the furniture restoration industry by removal men and cleaning ladies.

Biscuit jointers – good or bad?

On the construction and jointing techniques front, I do have a problem with biscuit jointers and although I possess a fine biscuit jointer, I am a very reluctant user. It can't be the noise and dust biscuit jointers make I object to,

because I am a regular and enthusiastic router user. They are just as antisocial and, after all, I do possess dust extraction and a fine pair of orange ear defenders. My problem may stem from the fact that in furniture restoration there is little scope for the use of a biscuit jointer. The one possible use – for re-jointing tops – is not to be advised because there is a chance the swelling of the biscuit, when glued, will telegraph through to the surface. Evenly spaced elliptical bumps along the joints in an antique table top could look quite fetching but I don't think they would

"On the construction and jointing techniques front, I do have a problem with biscuit jointers and although I possess a fine biscuit jointer, I am a very reluctant user"

Simple and traditional jointing but very effective

Two through mortices, the tenons are formed by two sides of the column

Underside construction

Column base moulding

ever catch on in the trade!

Where the biscuit jointer really scores is with the professional cabinet maker who is trying to earn a crust and meet a client's budget. They do speed construction time up hugely and, as the Managing Editor of this fine publication will tell you, their structural integrity is beyond question, if used appropriately and intelligently. I don't have a problem with biscuits being used for jointing lumps of MDF together but using them in place of a mortice and tenon is obviously cheating.

A double biscuit, in place of a mortice and tenon, to my prehistoric brain, just doesn't look right and I don't think I'd ever be able to bring myself to execute one unless I was threatened with

extreme violence or a substantial financial incentive. All of which makes me think my feelings towards biscuit jointers are rather like my feelings towards Britain signing up for the single currency in Europe. If you look at it rationally it is beyond reasonable doubt a jolly good idea, but bring your heart into play and I want nothing to do with the nasty new fangled idea!

Luddite – me?

So I'm a dinosaur – it's official – but then that's probably why I was drawn to furniture restoration in the first place. I was always fascinated by the skills of the boys who made furniture 200/300 years ago. I also had a yearning to become a cabinetmaker but I wanted to

rely largely on hand skills not just be a skillful user of modern woodworking machinery. So that makes me an elitist dinosaur!

There's an American magazine I used to read before F&C came along and it certainly featured some fine pieces of woodworking but there was a definite preoccupation with using machines to do everything, by combining them with incredibly inventive jigs. But do you get a sense of achievement from developing your hand skills or from creating a jig that enables you to cut dovetails on a belt sander? In the end it's whatever turns you on, I suppose!

The danger is you can get too mesmerised with the use of machines to the point where you are sometimes ➤

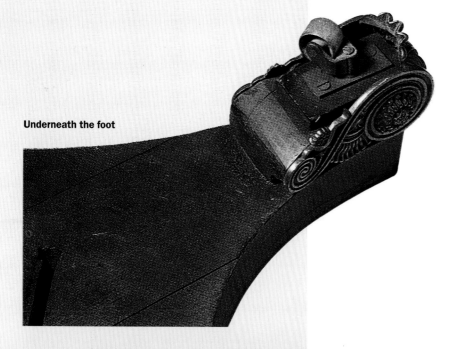

Underneath the foot

"It's very easy to get sucked into a machinery mindset, and I have often found myself trotting off to the machine shop to cut a small component on the bandsaw, when it would have been 10 times quicker – and more rewarding – to cut it with a hand saw!"

The inquisitiveness of a nine year old solved the mystery of how the foot was attached

Crossbanding of satin wood on the table top

losing time by using them. It's easy to get sucked into a machinery mindset and I have often found myself trotting off to the machine shop to cut a small component on the bandsaw, when it would have been 10 times quicker – and more rewarding – to cut it with a hand saw!

A furniture restorer is perhaps fortunate to be constantly reminded wonderful creations can be made using very simple constructional techniques that, to a large degree, stand the test of time because they are staring us in the face from the bench every day. We are also obliged to replicate damaged or missing bits which often have to be executed using traditional techniques to make them look right. With this

experience under our belts – and with a heated glue pot filled with Scotch glue in the corner – if we are making furniture we may naturally go for a simple construction using traditional methods and materials, rather than a modern approach which just might be more time consuming and/or possibly less fulfiling. Or it could just be that we've lost the instruction book for the biscuit jointer and are useless at making jigs?

Sofa tables – again

If you read and inwardly digested Chapter 7 of this book, you'll probably feel you already know enough about sofa tables to last you a very long time. But sofa tables are a bit like buses: you don't see one for ages, then two come

along at the same time. The main difference with this one is that the top is supported on a straight sided column rather than turned columns; it stands on feet rather than legs and it is veneered in rosewood in place of mahogany.

Renovation

The column had become loose at both the top and the bottom and – having persuaded it to part from the other bits – it gave me the opportunity to see one of the simplest of traditional construction methods. This consists of the four boards which form the sides of the column which were just glued together with butt joints and reinforced with glue blocks in the internal corners. These would have just been rub-jointed into place, and for rub joints you need smelly Scotch glue but you don't need cramps. The joints at the top and bottom of the column to joint it to the other components are mortice and tenon, and the tenons are formed by

Folding support, two of David Charlesworth's favourites here: a rule joint and a knuckle joint

Drawer detail with more satin wood crossbanding

"The main part of the top of this table had split in several places along the lines of the glue joints"

simply extending two opposite sides of the column.

The base is made up of boards running at right angles to each other which looks like a shrinkage problem just waiting to happen. But there were no visible splits in the veneer or the groundwork and the veneer running around the curved edges – which is glued to something very close to end grain – was also sound!

With the column removed from the base, it was also a good opportunity to see the original colour of the rosewood which had not been exposed to the light – it makes you wonder though why those Regency types got so excited about rosewood. I mean, what's so trendy about murky purple with black stripes? The column has a simple concave moulding around the base,

which, like the glue blocks, would have just been 'rubbed' into place using Scotch, quick and no pins or cramps required to hold it while the glue sets. The blocks forming the feet are just glued to the underside of the base but what did have me puzzled for a while was how the gilt mounts encasing the feet were fixed on? Luckily, my nine year old daughter paid me a visit in the workshop at the time I was pondering this question and while we were talking about something mundane like homework or the non appearance of her tea, I noticed she was playing with something; when asked what it was, she told me she had been twiddling it and it had, "just come off in her hands"! So the riddle was solved, the little circular patera had unscrewed from the

mounts to reveal the fixing screws beneath. Obvious really!

Damage

The main part of this table's top had split in several places along the lines of the glue joints. This is not an uncommon problem and was caused by shrinkage; the two splits on this top were each 2-3mm (³⁄₆₄-¹⁄₈in) wide. It isn't too difficult to glue these joints; the main challenge is to get the top surface accurately in register but before I started splashing glue around I assembled the top with the gaps closed up and checked it was still long enough to allow the flaps to hang vertically, when down. Flaps sticking out at an angle look silly and the table resembles some sort of deformed duck trying to get airborne. In this case the maker had obviously instinctively known central heating would be invented one day and had made an appropriate allowance in the length, but if it had been too short I would have had to insert a fillet into one of the splits to extend the top. Of course, if he'd been really clever he would have used MDF. But then who knows what state MDF will be in in 200 years! ∎

INDEX

A

adjustable shelves 47
animal glue 96, 98
ankle 107
Antique Collectors Club 75
antiquing brass 111
arm (of fly leg) 51–2
arrises 41, 106, 107

B

back legs 31
back plate 89
baize 52, 55, 81
baking parchment 44, 96
ball and claw foot 107
balloon back chairs **95**, 98
band cramps **5**, **96**, 97
bandsaw 31, 32, 51, 106
        for metal 80
banjo barometers 62
barometers 61–4
Basford Hall 18
beech 31, 50, 82
bench grinder 101
bendy–ply 102
Birkbeck, Ben 18
biscuit jointers 116–17
blanks 109
block plane 19
blocks 99
bobbin cutting 12
bookcase 46
bracket feet 88, 91–3
brass fittings 46, 48, 79–80, 111
Brazilian mahogany 31
breakers 74
bridle joints 4
broken pediment 63–4
bronze paint 114
bucket castors 110
bun feet 91–2, 105
bureau, copy of 18th c. **18**
burr elm 93
burr oak 75
butt joints 118
butterflies 10, **80**, 81

C

Cabinet Dictionary (Sheraton) 8
cabinet scraper 35, 106
cabinets 7–10, 104
cabriole 33
cabriole legs 85, **104**, 105–7
callipers 31
candle stands 39
caning 85
canted corners 59, 101–2
capitals 114
carcass
        splits **15**
card tables, fold–over 50–52, 53–5, 78
carving chisels 64, 69
Cascamite 44, 52, 55
central heating 49
chair backs 98
chair legs 31, 84
chairs 82–5, 95–8, 105
        Chippendale style carver
                                42–4
        history 85
        wobbly 98
chairs, copying 29–36
        assembly 35
        caning 35
        drawings 34, 36
        machining 31
        making drawings 29
        profiling 33
        veneering 35
Charles II 85, 104
chess boards 26
chest on chest 58–60, **90**, 93, 112

chest on stand **104**, 105
chest with cupboard 87
chests 90, 104
chests of drawers 15–17, 90–93
        history 91
chiffonier 45–8
        in England 46
        in France 45
chiffonier plinth 109–10
chiffonière 45
Chippendale style 11, 42–5
Chippendale, Thomas 86, 116
chisels 6
clavichord 20
cleats 53–4
Clementi, Muzio 21
clocks 112–15
        history 113
cockbeading 15, 18–19, 88
colour 26, 60
colouring 35, 93, 111
columns 114
compound curves 102
conservation 51, 58
console table 71–3
coopered column 102
cooperaring technique 4, 10
corner blocks 97
corner cupboard 56
cornice moulding 58–9
cornices 58, 89
counter veneering 53
cramping 16, 59–60, 93, 95–8, 99–102
cramping flats 98
cramps 118, 119
cranked chisel **6**, 69
cresting rail 33, 43, 97–8
Cromwell, Oliver 104
cross–banding 6, 79
cross–grain moulding 77
cross grain plugs 5
cross grained veneers 47
curved facing 4
cutter making 12, 114–15
cutting metal
        band saw 80
        junior hacksaw 79
cylinder 7–10, 7
        construction 9–10
        opening and closing 10
cylinder mechanism 10

D

dating furniture 75
Davenport, Captain 87
Davenport desks 87, **105**
dealing with clients 70–71, 78, 90
demi–lune table see tea–tables
denim jeans 102
dental moulding compound
                                12, 114, **113**
dismantling furniture
        9, 26–7, 38, 68, 77, 83–4
dog–leg chisel *see* cranked chisel
doors 46–4, 56, **87**
dovetail insert 76
dovetails 28, 39, 93, **27**, **41**
dowel plates 41
dowels 41, 82
drawer fronts 101–2
drawer rail 16
drawer runners 15–16, 100
drawer sides 93
drawers 15–17, 18–19, 88, 104
drawings 29
drill bits 5
drills 111
drop handles 111
drop–in seats 82, 85
drop–leaf tables 68
dry run 97
dummy drawer front 111
dustboard 16

E

East India Company 39
ebonized moulding 76–7
ebonizing 77
Edwardian furniture 75
eighteenth century 91
England 46
epoxy resin 43
Evelyn, John 3
extending leaves 26

F

F–cramps 96
feet 26, 46, 88, 90–93, 105, 119
fence for band saw 51
fillets 10, 119
finials 63–4
finishing 60, 64, 73, 77, 115
fish glue 114
fixing screws 119
flaps 25, 69, 119
flat stretchers 105
flattening 51–2, 53–6
        router jig **54**, 55
fly brackets 26, 28
fly–legs 50–52
folding tops **38**, 39
formaldehyde 98
formers 14
Forstner bit 111
frame and panel construction
                        49, 56, 90, 104
France 11, 45
fretwork 58
frieze drawers 26, 76
friezes 4, 28, 76, 80
front legs 31
Furniture and Cabinetmaking Magazine
                                116, 118
furniture marks 86

G

G–cramps 96, 99
Galileo 61
gated legs 4
Georgian furniture 86
gilding 89, 114
Gillow, Robert 87
Gillows of Lancaster 86
gilt fittings 26, 113–14, 119
glue blocks 89, 118–19
glues 52, 84
go–bars 16, 100
grand piano 21
grandfather clock
        see longcase clock
guide bush 27

H

hacksaw 115
handles 60, 89, 111
hardener 73
Harlequin Pembroke table 66
harpsichords 20
Henry VIII 20
Hepplewhite, George 8, 86
hessian 83
hide glue 9
hinged top 4
hinges **5**, 6, 67–9, 79
        binding 69
home made cramps 96
hood 113
hot air gun 98
housing joint 92
housings 40
hygrometer 62

I

inner tubes 44, 96, 101, **102**

irons 81, 96, 100
Italy 11, 71
ivory 63

J

Japanese saw 16, 18
jigs 117
'joyned' chair 85
junior hacksaw 12, 79
Jupes 66

K

kerfed MDF 102
knobs 111
knuckle joints 28, 51, 119

L

laminates 42–4
laminating 51
Lancaster 87
leg base joints 27–8
leg splice 84
leg to column joint 38
legs 4, 109–11
        loose 4–5
        screw in 22–3
        splits in 4–5
linen cupboard 87
linen presses 104
linenfold panels 85
lion's paw feet 26
lip–moulding 18
London 21
long reach cramps 96, 99
longcase clock 112–15
loose joints 5, 27, 82, 109

M

Macassar ebony 26
machine use 117–118
mahogany 26, 49, 118
man–made boards *see also* MDF 50
marquetry **10**
masking tape 6, 13–14, 100–101
MDF 50, 55, 116, 117
MDF pads 107
mercury filled glass tube 62
metal brackets 82
metalwork
        cleaning 48
Middle Ages 85
mitre support block 91–2
mitres 71
modern equipment and materials 116
mortice and tenon 83–5, 117, 118–19
mortice gauge 31
morticer 28
mortices 28, 31
mould 71
mould making 114
mouldings 71, 76–77, 114–15, 119
        attaching 13–14
        dentil 58–9
        ogee 47, **48**
        split & turned
                        11–13, 25, 47, **48**
mule chest 91
muntin 75
musical boxes 20
musical instruments 20

N

Nitromors Craftsman 43

O

oak 75
oak furniture 49
original surfaces 43, 84
Oxford Street, London 87

P

pad foot 107
paint stripper 73
panel saw 31
Paraloid 114
patches 5
patera 63, 89, 119
patina 13
pearl glue 98, 114
pedestal 25
Pembroke, Countess of 66
Pembroke tables 25, 66–9, 108–11
pendulum 113
Pennant, Thomas 87
pet damage 108–9
piano 20
pianoforte 21
pie–crust edging 40
pier glass 72
pier table 71–3
piercing metal 80
piercing saw 59
pillar
      split 39–41
pinning 19
plaster 114
Plasticine 12, 71
platform bases 11
plinths 114
plugs 5
ply 55
polishing 35
polyester filler 114
polystyrene 102
power fret saw 59
PVA 9, 81

Q

quadrant drawer slips 75
quarter sawn timber 49
Queen Anne style 105

R

refinishing 78
Regency style 11, 26, 46, 78, 91
release agent wax 114
restoration 57–8, 74
Restoration period 11, 104
reversibility 84, 114

reversible head cramp 83
riven timber 49
rosewood 11, 26, 47, 71, 118–19
router jig 77
      for flattening **54**, 55
routers **8**, 17, 27, 55, **67**, 68, 69
rub joints 93, 118, 119
rule joints 67–9, 119
runners 15–16, 100

S

'S' shape 64
sand bags 102
sand–paper 107
sash cramps
    60, 84, 95, 96, 97, 100, 102, 107
saw kerfing 53
saw tooth cutter 111
scarfe joints 6, 44, 80
Scotch glue 17, 81, 84, 93, 118, 119
scratch stock 11415
screw box 22
screw holes 5
screws 68, 82
scribing a profile 115
scrolls 63–4
seat rails 32, 82, 97, 98
secret compartments 88–9
secretaire drawer 87, 88–9
seventeenth century 11, 91
shaped blocks 101–2
shaping 35, 106–7
shelf assembly 48
shellac 114
Sheppy Tug 98
Sheraton, Thomas
    3, 8, 25, 46, 66, 72, 86, 95
shooting board 19
Shorter Dictionary of English
    Furniture 3
shoulder plane 69, 71
shrinkage 49–50, 59, 77, 119
side rails 32
signature 4
simulated ivory 63
sixteenth century 11
skew chisel 63, **68**
skew gouge 12
Skilsaw 31
sliding carriage 32

Smith, George 46
Smith, John 113
sockets 110–11, **26**
sofa tables 25–8, 67, 118–19
    history 25–6
softening blocks 96–7, 100
softening glue 38, 43, 51, 83
softwood 73
spigots 109–10
spindle moulder 114
spinets 20–21
splats 29, 33, 42–4
splices 84, 85, 93
splits 4–5, 15, 39–41, 77, 81, 119
spokeshave 35, 106
spokeshaving **105**
spring clamps 101, **102**
square piano **20**, 21–3
steam bending 13
steam machine **76**, 77
stick barometers 62
stile feet 90
stretcher 25
stretcher rail, turned 75
stringing 6, 80
stuff–over seats 29, 82, 85
sunlight 60
support column 118–19
Sutherland table 66

T

table hinges 67
table tops 26–7, 116
    baize 52, 55, 81
    bowed 69
    cramping 99
    figured **51**
    refinishing 72–73
    split 40, 77, 81, 119
    warped 53–5, 78
Taiwan 22
taking casts 114
tall boy 112
tambour 7–10
    construction 8–9
    glueing jig **8**
    repair 9
tea drinking 39
tea–tables 3–6, 38–41
templates 29, 31, 93, 106

tenons *see also* mortice and tenon
    32, 35, 85, **110**, 111
thermometer 62
tongues 4
Toricelli, Evangelista 61
traditional methods 118
trimming 18, 81
tripod tables 38–41
trunks 90
turned legs 105, 109–11
turning 12–13, 31, 63, 110

U

upholstery 82
upholstery springs **17**, 96, 101
upright piano 21

V

V & A museum 114
veneer 56, 73, 78, **87**, 88, 102
    repairing 6
veneer banding 100–101
veneer pins 19
Victorian furniture 74–5
Victorian period 47, 95
virginals 20

W

'wainscot' chair 85
wallpaper paste 81
walnut 85, 106
warding files 80, 115
wax 114
wedges 27, 83, 96
weights 60, 100
wind surfer straps 96
wood identification 70–71
wooden bars 99
wooden screw threads 22–3
woodworm 51, 82
writing slide 45
writing tables 11–14, 66, 75–7
    early designs 14

Z

zebrawood 26

CONVERSION TABLE: INCHES TO MILLIMETRES

inch		mm	inch		mm	inch		mm
1/64	0.0565	0.3969	3/8	0.375	9.5250	47/64	0.734375	18.6531
1/32	0.03125	0.7938	25/64	0.390625	9.9219			
3/64	0.046875	1.1906	13/32	0.40625	10.3188	3/4	0.750	19.0500
1/16	0.0625	1.5875	27/64	0.421875	10.7156			
						49/64	0.765625	19.4469
5/64	0.078125	1.9844	7/16	0.4375	11.1125	25/32	0.78125	19.8438
3/32	0.09375	2.3812	29/64	0.453125	11.5094	51/64	0.796875	20.2406
7/64	0.109375	2.7781	15/32	0.46875	11.9062	13/16	0.8125	20.6375
			31/64	0.484375	12.3031			
1/8	0.125	3.1750				53/64	0.828125	21.0344
9/64	0.140625	3.5719	1/2	0.500	12.700	27/32	0.84375	21.0344
5/32	0.15625	3.9688	33/64	0.515625	13.0969	55/64	0.858375	21.8281
11/64	0.171875	4.3656	17/32	0.53125	13.4938			
			35/64	0.546875	13.8906	7/8	0.875	22.2250
3/16	0.1875	4.7625	9/16	0.5625	14.2875	57/64	0.890625	22.6219
13/64	0.203125	5.1594				29/32	0.90625	23.0188
7/32	0.21875	5.5562	37/64	0.578125	14.6844	59/64	0.921875	23.4156
15/64	0.234375	5.9531	19/32	0.59375	15.0812			
1/4	0.250	6.3500	39/64	0.609375	15.4781	15/16	0.9375	23.8125
						61/64	0.953125	24.2094
17/64	0.265625	6.7469	5/8	0.625	15.8750	31/32	0.96875	24.6062
9/32	0.28125	7.5406	41/64	0.640625	16.2719	63/64	0.984375	25.0031
5/16	0.3125	7.9375	21/32	0.65625	16.6688			
			43/64	0.671875	17.0656	**1**	**1.00**	**25.4**
21/64	0.1328125	8.3344	11/16	0.6875	17.4625			
11/32	0.34375	8.7312	45/64	0.703125	17.8594			
23/64	0.359375	9.1281	23/32	0.71875	18.2562			

WOODCARVING

The Art of the Woodcarver	GMC Publications
Beginning Woodcarving	GMC Publications
Carving Architectural Detail in Wood: The Classical Tradition	
	Frederick Wilbur
Carving Birds & Beasts	GMC Publications
Carving the Human Figure: Studies in Wood and Stone	Dick Onians
Carving Nature: Wildlife Studies in Wood	Frank Fox-Wilson
Carving Realistic Birds	David Tippey
Decorative Woodcarving	Jeremy Williams
Elements of Woodcarving	Chris Pye
Essential Woodcarving Techniques	Dick Onians
Lettercarving in Wood: A Practical Course	Chris Pye
Making & Using Working Drawings for Realistic Model Animals	
	Basil F. Fordham
Power Tools for Woodcarving	David Tippey
Relief Carving in Wood: A Practical Introduction	Chris Pye
Understanding Woodcarving	GMC Publications
Understanding Woodcarving in the Round	GMC Publications
Useful Techniques for Woodcarvers	GMC Publications
Wildfowl Carving – Volume 1	Jim Pearce
Wildfowl Carving – Volume 2	Jim Pearce
Woodcarving: A Complete Course	Ron Butterfield
Woodcarving: A Foundation Course	Zoë Gertner
Woodcarving for Beginners	GMC Publications
Woodcarving Tools & Equipment Test Reports	GMC Publications
Woodcarving Tools, Materials & Equipment	Chris Pye

WOODTURNING

Adventures in Woodturning	David Springett
Bert Marsh: Woodturner	Bert Marsh
Bowl Turning Techniques Masterclass	Tony Boase
Colouring Techniques for Woodturners	Jan Sanders
Contemporary Turned Wood: New Perspectives in a Rich Tradition	
	Ray Leier, Jan Peters & Kevin Wallace
The Craftsman Woodturner	Peter Child
Decorating Turned Wood: The Maker's Eye	Liz & Michael O'Donnell
Decorative Techniques for Woodturners	Hilary Bowen
Fun at the Lathe	R.C. Bell
Illustrated Woodturning Techniques	John Hunnex
Intermediate Woodturning Projects	GMC Publications
Keith Rowley's Woodturning Projects	Keith Rowley
Making Screw Threads in Wood	Fred Holder
Turned Boxes: 50 Designs	Chris Stott
Turning Green Wood	Michael O'Donnell
Turning Miniatures in Wood	John Sainsbury
Turning Pens and Pencils	Kip Christensen & Rex Burningham
Understanding Woodturning	Ann & Bob Phillips
Useful Techniques for Woodturners	GMC Publications
Useful Woodturning Projects	GMC Publications
Woodturning: Bowls, Platters, Hollow Forms, Vases,	
Vessels, Bottles, Flasks, Tankards, Plates	GMC Publications
Woodturning: A Foundation Course (New Edition)	Keith Rowley
Woodturning: A Fresh Approach	Robert Chapman
Woodturning: An Individual Approach	Dave Regester
Woodturning: A Source Book of Shapes	John Hunnex
Woodturning Jewellery	Hilary Bowen
Woodturning Masterclass	Tony Boase
Woodturning Techniques	GMC Publications
Woodturning Tools & Equipment Test Reports	GMC Publications
Woodturning Wizardry	David Springett

WOODWORKING

Advanced Scrollsaw Projects	GMC Publications
Beginning Picture Marquetry	Lawrence Threadgold
Bird Boxes and Feeders for the Garden	Dave Mackenzie
Complete Woodfinishing	Ian Hosker
David Charlesworth's Furniture–Making Techniques	David Charlesworth
David Charlesworth's Furniture–Making Techniques – Volume 2	
	David Charlesworth
The Encyclopedia of Joint Making	Terrie Noll

Furniture–Making Projects for the Wood Craftsman	GMC Publications
Furniture–Making Techniques for the Wood Craftsman	GMC Publications
Furniture Projects	Rod Wales
Furniture Restoration (Practical Crafts)	Kevin Jan Bonner
Furniture Restoration: A Professional at Work	John Lloyd
Furniture Restoration and Repair for Beginners	Kevin Jan Bonner
Furniture Restoration Workshop	Kevin Jan Bonner
Green Woodwork	Mike Abbott
The History of Furniture	Michael Huntley
Intarsia: 30 Patterns for the Scrollsaw	John Everett
Kevin Ley's Furniture Projects	Kevin Ley
Making & Modifying Woodworking Tools	Jim Kingshott
Making Chairs and Tables	GMC Publications
Making Chairs and Tables – Volume 2	GMC Publications
Making Classic English Furniture	Paul Richardson
Making Heirloom Boxes	Peter Lloyd
Making Little Boxes from Wood	John Bennett
Making Screw Threads in Wood	Fred Holder
Making Shaker Furniture	Barry Jackson
Making Woodwork Aids and Devices	Robert Wearing
Mastering the Router	Ron Fox
Minidrill: Fifteen Projects	John Everett
Pine Furniture Projects for the Home	Dave Mackenzie
Practical Scrollsaw Patterns	John Everett
Router Magic: Jigs, Fixtures and Tricks to	
Unleash your Router's Full Potential	Bill Hylton
Router Tips & Techniques	GMC Publications
Routing: A Workshop Handbook	Anthony Bailey
Routing for Beginners	Anthony Bailey
The Scrollsaw: Twenty Projects	John Everett
Sharpening: The Complete Guide	Jim Kingshott
Sharpening Pocket Reference Book	Jim Kingshott
Simple Scrollsaw Projects	GMC Publications
Space–Saving Furniture Projects	Dave Mackenzie
Stickmaking: A Complete Course	Andrew Jones & Clive George
Stickmaking Handbook	Andrew Jones & Clive George
Storage Projects for the Router	GMC Publications
Test Reports: The Router and Furniture & Cabinetmaking	GMC Publications
Veneering: A Complete Course	Ian Hosker
Veneering Handbook	Ian Hosker
Woodfinishing Handbook (Practical Crafts)	Ian Hosker
Woodworking with the Router: Professional	
Router Techniques any Woodworker can Use	Bill Hylton & Fred Matlack
The Workshop	Jim Kingshott

MAGAZINES

WOODTURNING ◆ WOODCARVING ◆ THE ROUTER
WOODWORKING ◆ FURNITURE & CABINETMAKING
THE DOLLS' HOUSE MAGAZINE ◆ BUSINESSMATTERS
WATER GARDENING ◆ OUTDOOR PHOTOGRAPHY
BLACK & WHITE PHOTOGRAPHY